# MAKING WAVES

# Other Boston Children's Museum Activity Books by Bernie Zubrowski

**Balloons:**
Building and Experimenting with Inflatable Toys

**Ball-Point Pens**

**Blinkers and Buzzers:**
Building and Experimenting with Electricity and Magnetism

**Bubbles**

**Clocks:**
Building and Experimenting with Model Timepieces

**Messing Around with Drinking Straws**

**Messing Around with Water Pumps**

**Milk Carton Blocks**

**Mirrors:**
Finding Out About the Properties of Light

**Mobiles:**
Building and Experimenting with Balancing Toys

**Raceways:**
Having Fun with Balls and Tracks

**Tops:**
Building and Experimenting with Spinning Toys

**Wheels at Work:**
Building and Experimenting with Models of Machines

# MAKING WAVES
## FINDING OUT ABOUT RHYTHMIC MOTION

**BERNIE ZUBROWSKI**

ILLUSTRATED BY **ROY DOTY**

A BOSTON CHILDREN'S MUSEUM ACTIVITY BOOK

A BEECH TREE PAPERBACK BOOK • NEW YORK

First Beech Tree Edition, 1994.
ISBN 0-688-11788-0

Printed in the United States of America.

1   2   3   4   5   6   7   8   9   10

The Library of Congress has cataloged the Morrow Junior Books edition of Making Waves as follows:
Zubrowski, Bernie.   Making waves: finding out about rhythmic motion / Bernie Zubrowski; illustrated by Roy Doty.
p.   cm. — (Boston Children's Museum activity book)
1. Waves—Juvenile literature.   [1. Waves—Experiments.   2. Experiments.]   I. Doty, Roy, ill.   II. Title.   III. Series.
QC157.Z83   1994   532'.0593—dc20   93-35455   CIP   AC

## Acknowledgments

Thanks to Gary Goldstein, who checked the accuracy of the scientific content, and extra-special thanks to Marjorie Waters, who helped me put the final manuscript into clear and coherent form. Also to the students at the Farragut and Hennigan schools of Boston, and the Phillips School of Watertown, Massachusetts, who helped try out the projects in this book.

# CONTENTS

# INTRODUCTION

When you think about waves, you may think first about waves in water: the ocean crashing onto the beach, or the ripples on a pond, or the wake behind a boat. You can also see smaller waves in bathtubs and puddles and pots of boiling water. The patterns of these watery waves are interesting and fun to watch, and they are very similar to one another, no matter how big the body of water is.

Other materials wave, too: flags on flagpoles, fields of tall grass, and sheets and towels hung outside on a clothesline. During a hurricane, trees and tall buildings will wave, and even the earth moves in a wavelike pattern during an earthquake.

Knowing how waves travel through different kinds of materials can be helpful in understanding many kinds of phenomena. Scientists

have applied this knowledge to understand how sound and light travel. They have even used it to learn about the smallest unit of matter, the atom.

The devices you build in this book and the experiments you play around with will help you begin to understand some of the basic properties of waves. As you explore, you can enjoy the beautiful movement of waves in different materials, both liquid and solid, and at the same time learn how scientists have come to describe their properties.

Most of the materials you will need for your projects are probably already around your house or classroom. You may have to buy a few items, though. If you do, the materials list for each project will suggest where you can purchase them.

Some of the projects will also require care and patience. You may not get them to work the first time you try. Keep trying and varying what you do, and review the instructions.

# WAVES IN LIQUIDS

In the following activities, you will be creating some waves of your own and seeing how the waves change when you make different kinds of disturbances and change the depth of the water.

## MAKING WAVES: FINGER POWER

If you have ever been at a beach on a windy day, you know one thing for sure: Ocean waves can be huge and powerful. You probably think that the bigger the body of water, the bigger the waves—and you're right. Even so, waves are waves, and they are similar whether they're in the ocean or in a puddle.

Because of this principle, you will learn a lot about waves in general by watching how water moves in a small tank. And you will be able to play around with the elements that cause waves to form, change, and disappear, in order to see what happens.

## MAKING A TEST TANK

The tank you will be using for this exploration should be wide, shallow, and transparent. The best choice for a tray is a plastic picture frame, at least 18 inches by 24 inches, with edges that are no less than $\frac{1}{2}$ inch high.

½ TO 1 INCH HIGH

CLEAR PLASTIC TRAY

18 INCHES

24 INCHES

These large trays can be found at some photo supply and photo developing stores. But if you can't find one, don't worry. A good watertight tank is easy to make.

You will need:

      1 piece of Plexiglas, 18 inches long, 24 inches wide, and $\frac{1}{8}$ inch thick

      1 package of oil-based clay, such as Plasticine

      water

Step 1.   Shape the clay into 4 strips. The strips should be about $\frac{1}{2}$ inch thick, $\frac{1}{2}$ inch wide, and as long as the sides of the Plexiglas.

Step 2.   Press the strips of clay tightly along the edges of the Plexiglas. Make sure they meet at the corners. Keep going until there is a border of clay all the way around the edges of the Plexiglas.

Step 3.   Pinch the clay so it stands upright and makes a wall about 1 inch high.

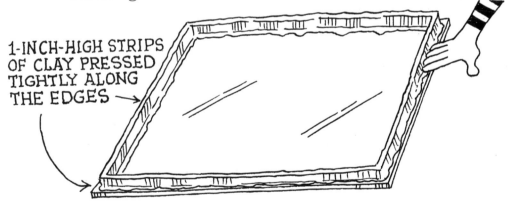

1-INCH-HIGH STRIPS OF CLAY PRESSED TIGHTLY ALONG THE EDGES →

Step 4.   To test the seal between the clay and the Plexiglas, add about $\frac{1}{4}$ inch of water to the tank. If you see any leaks, press the clay more tightly against the Plexiglas. Once you are sure your tank is watertight, empty out the water.

# MAKING THE OVERHEAD LIGHT

In this exploration, a flashlight bulb serves as a tiny sun and casts reflections on the floor below the tank. (The light uses very little power. There is no danger of a shock.)

You will need:

> 1 7.2-volt flashlight bulb
>
> 1 piece of thin-wall plastic tubing, 1 inch long by $\frac{1}{2}$ inch in diameter (This is available at most hardware stores.)
>
> 1 nail, 2 inches long
>
> 2 pieces of flexible electrical wire, each about 3 feet long (This is sold by the roll at most hardware stores or at Radio Shack.)
>
> 1 battery holder for 4 D-size batteries (This is available at Radio Shack or a hobby shop.)

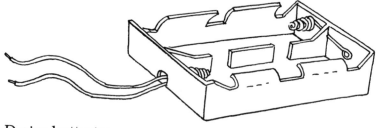

4 D-size batteries
knife

Step 1.  Push the nail through the middle of the plastic tubing.

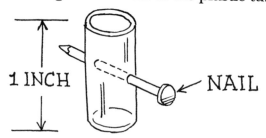

1 INCH          NAIL

**Step 2.** With a knife, *carefully* strip the insulation off the ends of both pieces of electrical wire so that about 1 inch of metal wiring is exposed at each end.

**Step 3.** Wrap a bare end of wire around the head of the nail.

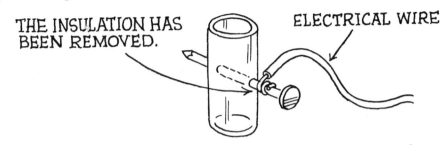

THE INSULATION HAS BEEN REMOVED.

ELECTRICAL WIRE

**Step 4.** Take the other piece of electrical wire and put about $\frac{1}{2}$ inch of the bare end inside the tubing.

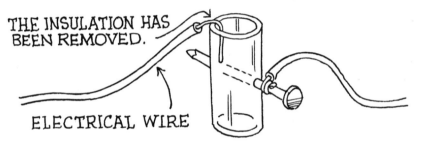

THE INSULATION HAS BEEN REMOVED.

ELECTRICAL WIRE

Slide the metal base of the flashlight bulb into the tubing until the tip touches the nail. Make sure the wire does not touch the nail. It should be held in place by the bulb.

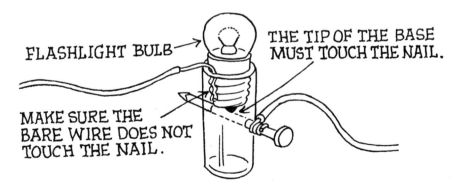

FLASHLIGHT BULB

THE TIP OF THE BASE MUST TOUCH THE NAIL.

MAKE SURE THE BARE WIRE DOES NOT TOUCH THE NAIL.

Step 5.   To test your light, put 4 D-size batteries in the battery holder.
Connect the free ends of the 2 pieces of electrical wire to the
battery holder, as shown. The bulb should light.

2 WIRES FROM BULB
HOLDER CONNECTED TO
2 WIRES FROM BATTERY
HOLDER

# MAKING A STAND FOR THE OVERHEAD LIGHT

You will need:

4 dowels, each 36 inches long and $\frac{1}{4}$ inch in diameter
2 rubber bands

Step 1.   Hold the 4 dowels together and wrap the rubber bands
around them about 3 inches from an end. Spread the other
ends of the dowels apart and position them just inside the
corners of the tank.

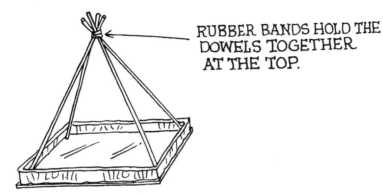

RUBBER BANDS HOLD THE
DOWELS TOGETHER
AT THE TOP.

# SETTING UP THE TEST TANK AND OVERHEAD LIGHT

You will need:

      2 chairs or tables of the same height

      2 yardsticks

Step 1.   Place the tables or chairs about 20 inches apart.

Step 2.   Set down the tank so the ends are supported by the tables or chairs. If you use a picture frame, you will not need extra support to keep it from sagging. But a homemade Plexiglas tank may twist and spill. Therefore, before you set down this type of tank, put 2 yardsticks between the tables or chairs and position the tank on them.

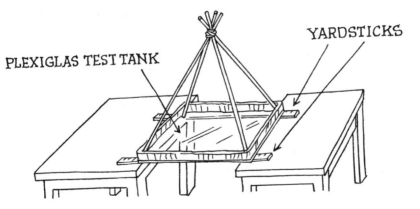

YARDSTICKS

PLEXIGLAS TEST TANK

# GETTING STARTED

Before you can start your exploration of waves, you must set up your tank.

You will need:

> 1 piece of unlined white paper, about 24 inches long and
>    20 inches wide
>
> water

Step 1.    Place the battery holder on one of the tables or chairs. Hang the overhead light from the top of the stand by wrapping each of the electrical wires around a dowel.

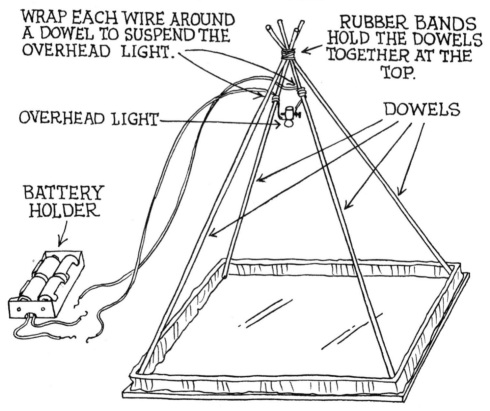

WRAP EACH WIRE AROUND A DOWEL TO SUSPEND THE OVERHEAD LIGHT.

RUBBER BANDS HOLD THE DOWELS TOGETHER AT THE TOP.

OVERHEAD LIGHT

DOWELS

BATTERY HOLDER

Step 2.  Connect the battery-holder wires to the light-bulb wires.

Step 3.  Add water to the tray until it is about $\frac{1}{4}$ inch deep.

Step 4.  Place the piece of white paper on the floor beneath the tank. (This will make it easier to see the reflections of the waves.)

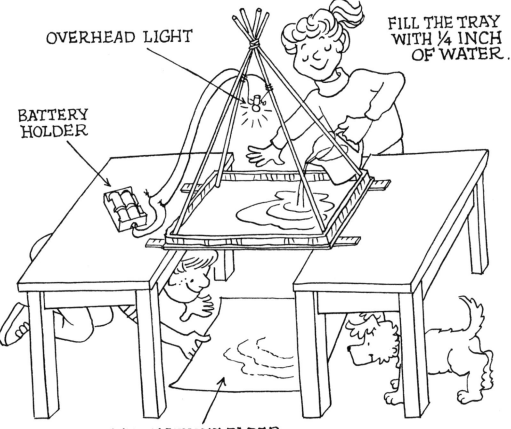

OVERHEAD LIGHT

FILL THE TRAY WITH ¼ INCH OF WATER.

BATTERY HOLDER

LARGE PIECE OF WHITE PAPER

Step 5.  Darken the room. Put a finger in the water and wiggle it a little. You should be able to see waves in the water and shadowy patterns on the paper below. These patterns will look like the ones you can see on the bottom of a pond on a sunny day. Sometimes it's easier to observe the shadows of waves than the waves themselves.

To perform the following experiments, you will need:

    2 12-inch rulers

    3 or 4 pieces of metal strapping or flexible metal, each
        12 inches long and $\frac{3}{4}$ inch wide (This is often found lying
        around lumberyards. It is used to hold bundles of wood
        planks together. Ask at a lumberyard for scrap pieces.)

    notebook

    pen or pencil

**Experiments to Try**

When you wiggle your finger on the surface of the water, a circular or semicircular wave pattern immediately appears on the white paper below. But if you put a ruler in the water and wiggle it gently with your fingers, you see *line*, or straight, waves reflected on the paper, not circular ones.

Play around with the water for a while and see how many different kinds of wave patterns you can make with your finger and the ruler. Also watch to see what happens when waves combine with one another or bump into something.

Remember to make drawings of each new pattern you observe, and write down how you made it happen. This will be helpful later to use for comparisons when you make waves with other kinds of materials.

Now try these experiments and see what happens.

• Blow on the surface of the water with a long, steady breath. What wave movements do you see reflected on the paper below the tank?

- Blow on the surface of the water in short puffs. Vary the force of the puffs and how long you blow. Do these variations cause the wave pattern to be different?
- Change the speed with which you wiggle a finger in the water. Does this change the pattern of the waves?
- Wiggle a finger from each hand in the water at the same time. Vary the speed at which you move the 2 fingers. Put them close together and wiggle them; move them several inches apart and try again. Put the 2 fingers at opposite ends of the tank and wiggle them.

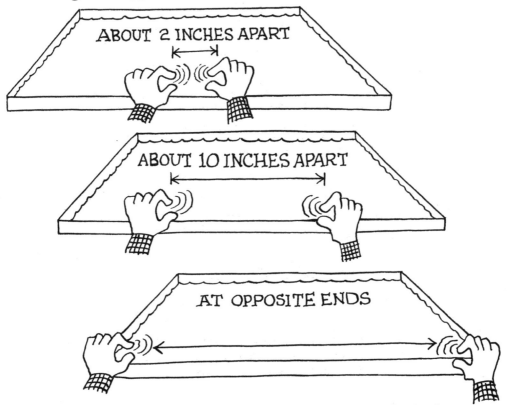

What do these changes in the speed and position of your fingers do to the waves?
- Poke your finger in the water once. What do you see? Keep poking with a steady rhythm. Then what do you see?

Now try the same explorations using a ruler instead of a finger.

- Let the ruler float on the surface of the water. Try tapping it from above. What pattern is produced? Next, move it back and forth on the surface and observe the waves.
- Hold 2 rulers upright and parallel to each other, with the ends in the water. Move the rulers up and down together, quickly and rhythmically. What patterns are produced?
- Move the rulers closer together and then farther apart. How does the distance change the waves? Next, keep the distance the same and change the position of the rulers so that they form a right angle to each other. How many different kinds of patterns can you make by varying the placement of the 2 rulers?
- With your hand, tap on the edge of the tank or the table or chairs supporting it. Use enough force so that you make the entire tank shake. What kind of wave patterns do you see?
- Bend a piece of metal strapping into a semicircle and put it in the middle of the tank. Put a finger in the water about 2 inches from this strapping and wiggle the finger.

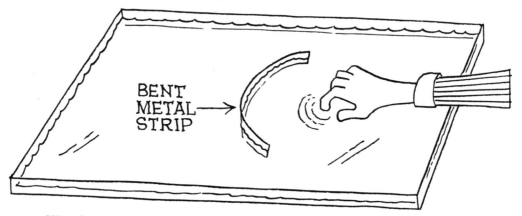

BENT METAL → STRIP

Watch carefully as the waves travel to the metal and are *reflected*, or bounced back. The waves may be faint and appear quickly, so do this several times to get a clear picture of what is happening.

• Lay the ruler in the water just at the opening of the semicircle. Tap the ruler and watch how line waves reflect off the metal.

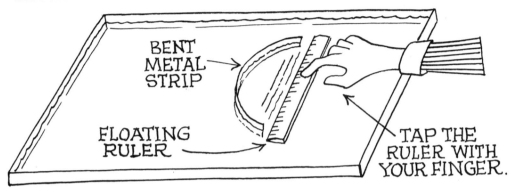

BENT METAL STRIP

FLOATING RULER

TAP THE RULER WITH YOUR FINGER.

Metal strapping is flexible and can be bent into different shapes. Try forming the metal strips into shapes like the ones in the drawings, or make up your own shapes. Then see how waves reflect from them.

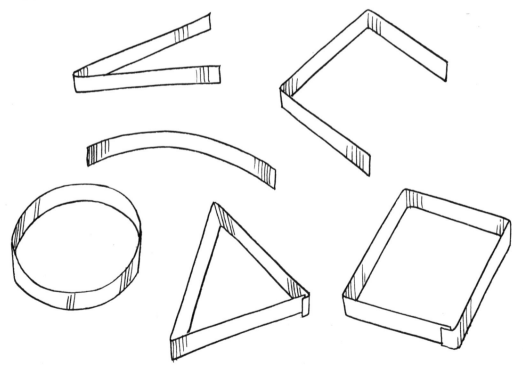

## What's Happening?

Blowing on the water disturbs the surface and creates waves. The pattern the waves make depends on how hard and long you blow, and where you are when you blow. A long, steady breath will probably make line waves, and short puffs of breath will probably make circular waves. If you hold your face over the water and blow straight down, you are likely to see circular waves. If you put your face close to the edge of the tank and blow across the water, you are more likely to see line waves.

When you wiggle a finger in the water, the wave pattern is just a series of circles that grow larger and larger in diameter as they move away from your finger. The faster you wiggle your finger, the closer the circles are to one another. The slower you wiggle your finger, the farther apart they are. No matter how fast or slow your finger goes, or whether you wiggle it intermittently or rhythmically, the resulting wave pattern is still a series of circles.

When you wiggle 2 fingers, you create 2 circular patterns. When these waves travel across one another, they form a series of diamond shapes. When your fingers are far apart, there is still a diamondlike pattern, but it will be faint and difficult to see.

Wiggling the ruler in the water or tapping it from above results in line patterns. If you wiggle 2 rulers together, the pattern may look like a checkerboard or a series of triangles, depending on the angle between the rulers.

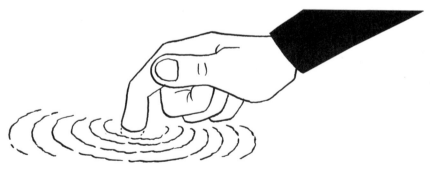

Two upright rulers moved up and down rhythmically produce a wave pattern similar to that of 2 moving fingers. Even though the rulers have straight edges, the resulting waves become circular very quickly because the waves are small in size.

The shape of waves also depends on what they bump into as they move through the water. When circular waves bump into one another and cross, they make a new pattern. You can duplicate this on paper. Use a compass to draw a series of circles. Then draw another series of circles overlapping the first set.

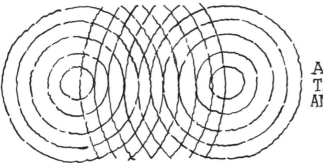

AS CIRCULAR WAVES TRAVEL PAST ONE ANOTHER, DIAMOND PATTERNS ARE FORMED.

The overlapping area forms a repeating pattern of diamonds, like the pattern you made when you wiggled your fingers in the water.

You can do the same thing with straight lines. Draw a set of straight lines going in one direction. Draw another set of lines that crosses the first.

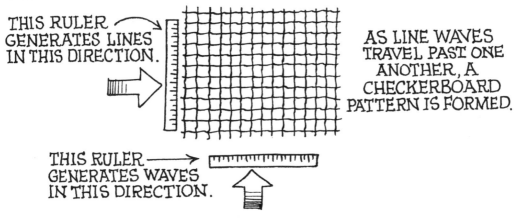

THIS RULER GENERATES LINES IN THIS DIRECTION.

AS LINE WAVES TRAVEL PAST ONE ANOTHER, A CHECKERBOARD PATTERN IS FORMED.

THIS RULER GENERATES WAVES IN THIS DIRECTION.

The overlapping area forms a checkerboard design like the one you saw when you held 2 rulers at right angles and wiggled them in the tank of water. It is also similar to the pattern that results when you shake the tank or tap its edge with a steady rhythm. The tank vibrates and sends out line waves from each side. The 4 lines of waves cross one another and form the checkerboard.

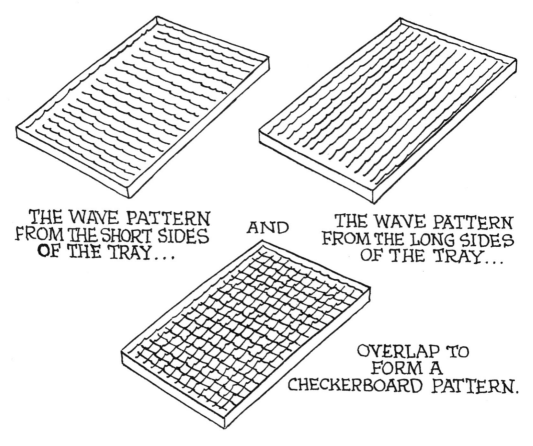

THE WAVE PATTERN FROM THE SHORT SIDES OF THE TRAY...

AND

THE WAVE PATTERN FROM THE LONG SIDES OF THE TRAY...

OVERLAP TO FORM A CHECKERBOARD PATTERN.

Waves will also change shape if they bump into an object in the water, and the shape of the new reflected waves will depend on the shape of the object. For example, when the piece of metal strapping is bent into a semicircle, it reflects circular waves, even if it is receiving line waves from a ruler. Circular or line waves reflecting off a metal

strip bent into a right angle will form a diamond-shaped pattern.
Waves reflecting off more complicated shapes create a more complex
pattern.

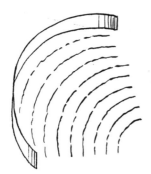

WAVES TRAVELING
TO A SEMICIRCULAR
METAL STRIP...

AND

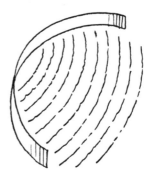

WAVES TRAVELING
FROM A SEMICIRCULAR
METAL STRIP...

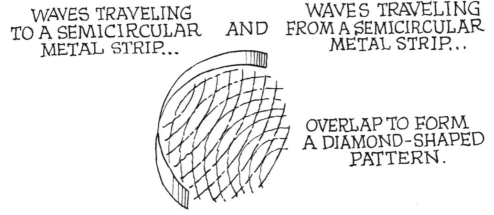

OVERLAP TO FORM
A DIAMOND-SHAPED
PATTERN.

Waves also change shape when they bump into the edges of the
container they are in.

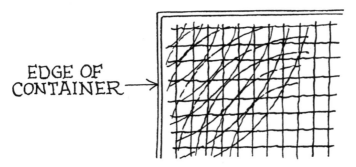

EDGE OF
CONTAINER →

From your explorations so far, you can draw some conclusions. Both the size and the shape of the objects making the waves determine what the waves will look like. Small round objects, such as your finger, a pencil, or the bottom of a can, will produce circular waves. Long or large objects with straight edges, such as a ruler or yardstick, will make line waves. However, smaller objects having straight edges will also give circular waves. The waves near these objects are not circular, but as they travel farther away, the waves become more and more circular.

Waves reflecting from walls or objects follow a similar pattern. Large curved walls or objects reflect back circular waves whether the incoming waves are curved or straight. Large flat walls reflect back circular waves from incoming circular waves and line waves from incoming line waves. When objects or walls have curves, bends, and angles, the resulting reflected waves are complex in their patterns.

In all these explorations, you do something—like wiggling your finger—that sends extra energy into the water and shakes up the flat surface. The extra energy pulls and stretches a small area of the water. This stretched part causes the neighboring region of the surface to be stretched also. The next region, in turn, is stretched, and this action continues onward. The extra energy that went into the water when your finger stretched the surface spreads out. As the *wave*, or rhythmic pattern, spreads outward, the extra energy is spreading over a larger area. This results in each successive wave having less energy. So the size of the wave gets smaller as it spreads outward, until it is hard to see at all.

What finally happens to that extra energy? It gets used up as the water both pushes against the bottom and sides of the tank and rubs against itself. A kind of friction uses up the extra energy, turning it into heat.

Another way that you can think about the spreading of wave energy is to compare it to a row of dominoes. Ordinarily, if you knock over the first domino in a long row, all of the others quickly fall over, having been pushed by the one in front of it. Now imagine that they are connected to each other with springs.

If you push the first one, it doesn't fall over, but it does pass on this energy to the next domino. Since they are all connected, this pulse of energy is carried on to each succeeding one. As the pulse travels along, each domino returns to its original standing position.

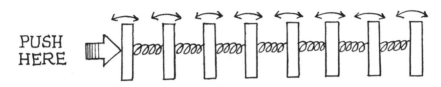

PUSH HERE

The waves in the tank are like the waves in the ocean. In certain situations along beaches, waves will sometimes form a regular pattern like the one shown in the photograph.

However, waves in the ocean or a lake are confusing to observe most of the time, so the tank gives you a small, controllable version of the wave movement you see in a big body of water. Your observations may seem very simple to you, but they are important. What you see happening in water is similar to what happens when other kinds of materials are disturbed. In later experiments, you will look at waves in some of these other materials.

# MAKING WAVES: MOTOR POWER

Wiggling your finger in water does make waves, but this technique limits the number of experiments you can do. Your finger gets tired, it doesn't wiggle at a constant speed, and it can go only as fast as your muscles can make it.

An alternative wave-maker is a device that uses an electric motor. With this, you can produce the same kind of disturbance for a long period of time, and you can vary the speed of the motor to see how this affects the wave pattern. The following sections show you how to make and use a wave generator. This device is worth the time and effort involved because you can use it for several explorations in this book.

## BUILDING THE WAVE GENERATOR

You will need:

> 1 piece of wood, 9 inches long, $5\frac{1}{2}$ inches wide, and about $\frac{3}{4}$ inch thick
>
> 8 wire nails with heads, 1 inch long
>
> 4 nails, $1\frac{1}{2}$ inches long
>
> 1 nail, 3 inches long
>
> 1 nail, 2 inches long
>
> 1 eraser pulled from the top of a new pencil

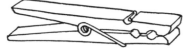

> 1 small 12-volt electric motor (This is available at Radio Shack or a hobby shop.)
>
> 1 clamp-type clothespin

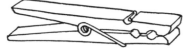

> knife

1 strip of metal, 4 inches long and $\frac{1}{2}$ inch wide (You can cut this from a soda can with scissors.)

1 piece of flexible electrical wire, 6 inches long

1 new bottle cork, about 1 inch long and $\frac{3}{4}$ inch in diameter (This is available at hardware stores. The cork must be *new*; do not use one from a wine bottle.)

1 battery holder for 4 D-size batteries

4 D-size batteries

1 fender washer, 1 inch in diameter

at least 4 rubber bands

at least 4 Popsicle sticks

Step 1.   Slide the 3-inch nail through the center of the metal spring of the clothespin.

SLIDE THE 3-INCH NAIL
THROUGH THE HOLE
OF THE SPRING.

Step 2.   Position the clothespin on the edge of the piece of wood so the clamp end extends beyond the wood about $\frac{1}{2}$ inch. The nail should rest on top of the wood.

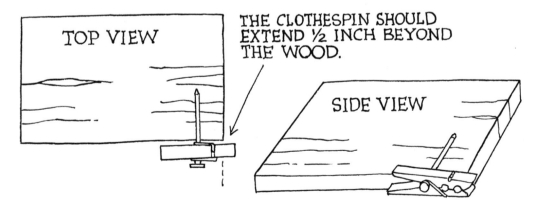

TOP VIEW

THE CLOTHESPIN SHOULD
EXTEND ½ INCH BEYOND
THE WOOD.

SIDE VIEW

Anchor the nail firmly to the wood by hammering the eight 1-inch nails on either side of it.

HAMMER 8 1-INCH
WIRE NAILS NEXT TO
THE 3-INCH NAIL TO
ANCHOR IT TIGHTLY
TO THE WOOD.

Step 3.   Push the eraser onto the shaft of the motor. The eraser should be slightly crooked on the shaft. You will have to do this carefully so the eraser does not split.

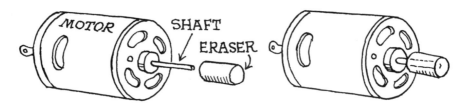

MOTOR   SHAFT   ERASER

Step 4.   Put the motor and the eraser on the piece of wood. Position them so that the eraser fits loosely into the opening formed by the 2 wooden handles of the clothespin. The eraser must be able to rotate quickly and make the clothespin vibrate.

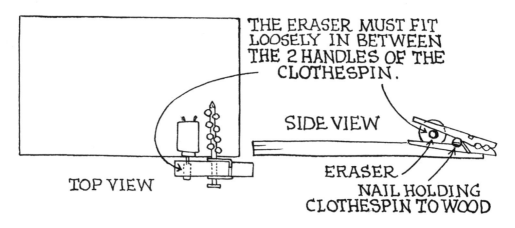

THE ERASER MUST FIT
LOOSELY IN BETWEEN
THE 2 HANDLES OF THE
CLOTHESPIN.

SIDE VIEW

TOP VIEW

ERASER

NAIL HOLDING
CLOTHESPIN TO WOOD

Step 5.   Secure the motor to the wood by hammering four $1\frac{1}{2}$-inch
          nails as shown. You can secure the motor more tightly by
          wrapping a rubber band around the nails to hold the motor
          in place.

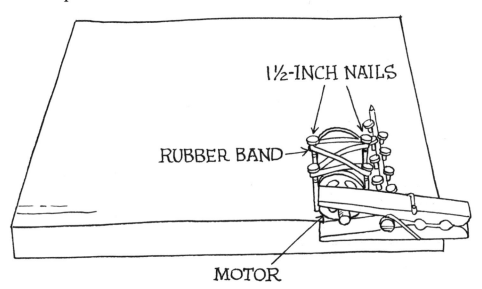

1½-INCH NAILS

RUBBER BAND

MOTOR

Step 6.   *Carefully* cut a slit in the side of the cork with a knife.

CUT A SLIT IN THE
SIDE OF A CORK.

CORK

Insert the narrow end of the metal strip into this slit.

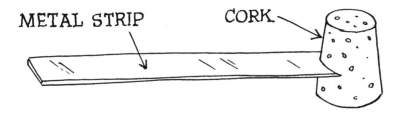

METAL STRIP

CORK

Put the other end of the metal strip into the clamp end of the clothespin.

ONE END OF THE METAL STRIP IS SLID INTO THE CLOTHESPIN.

CORK

CLOTHESPIN

Step 7.  Hammer the 2-inch nail into the wood on the same side as the motor but at the opposite end from it. Stretch a rubber band from this nail to the clothespin as shown. The rubber band should go through the clamp end of the clothespin so that it rests on the metal spring.

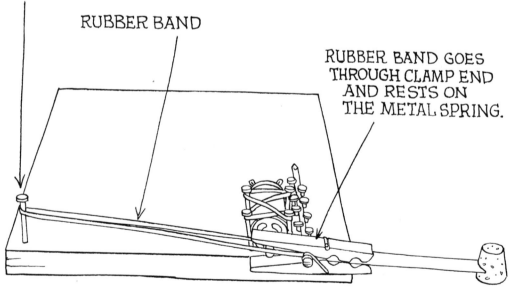

2-INCH NAIL

RUBBER BAND

RUBBER BAND GOES THROUGH CLAMP END AND RESTS ON THE METAL SPRING.

Step 8. Put 4 D-size batteries into the battery holder. Secure the battery holder to the wood with a rubber band as shown.

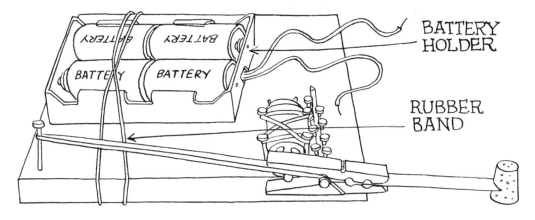

BATTERY HOLDER

RUBBER BAND

Step 9. Attach a battery-holder wire to a terminal of the motor. The other wire will not be attached to anything.

Step 10. Remove the insulation from both ends of a 6-inch piece of electrical wire. Attach an end of the wire to the other terminal of the motor. Wrap the other end of the wire around the washer.

WASHER

ONE END OF THE PIECE OF ELECTRICAL WIRE IS CONNECTED TO A MOTOR TERMINAL. THE OTHER END IS WRAPPED AROUND THE WASHER.

CONNECT 1 BATTERY HOLDER WIRE TO A MOTOR TERMINAL. THE OTHER BATTERY HOLDER WIRE IS LEFT UNCONNECTED.

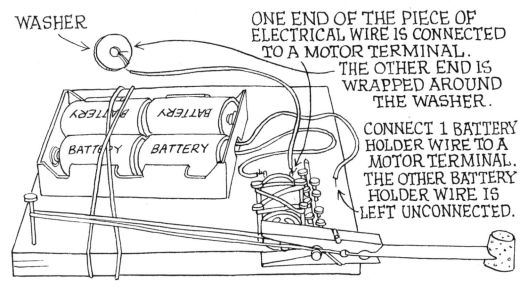

# USING THE WAVE GENERATOR

To turn on the wave generator, insert the washer in the battery holder. The washer is also used to control the amount of electricity the motor receives. When you put the washer in position 4 (see the illustration below), all 4 batteries will run the motor. If the washer is in position 3, then 3 batteries are operating. When the washer is inserted in positions 2 or 1, the motor is receiving electricity from 2 or 1 of the batteries. Therefore, by putting the washer in different positions, you can control the speed of the wave generator.

### POSITION 1

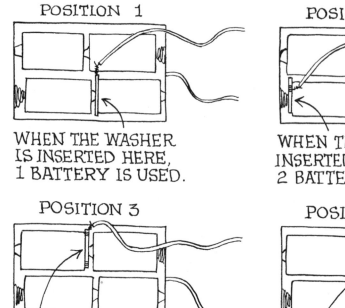

WHEN THE WASHER IS INSERTED HERE, 1 BATTERY IS USED.

### POSITION 2

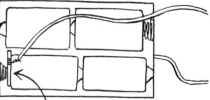

WHEN THE WASHER IS INSERTED AT THIS POSITION, 2 BATTERIES ARE USED.

### POSITION 3

THIS WASHER POSITION USES 3 BATTERIES.

### POSITION 4

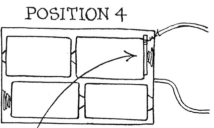

ALL 4 BATTERIES ARE BEING USED.

Start by inserting the washer in position 4. This is the wave generator's fastest speed. The most critical adjustment you may have to make is the space between the eraser and the opening in the clothespin. If there is enough room for the eraser to spin, it will cause the clothespin to rock up and down rapidly. If the clothespin doesn't

34

move at all, you have to position the motor so the eraser spins freely.

Experiment with the different wave-generator speeds by inserting the washer into the other positions. Positions 1 and 2 are slow, and you may have to wiggle the clothespin or the motor a little to get the wave generator started. Also make sure that the end of the metal strip is inserted firmly in the cork and can move up and down freely.

You can also change the speed of the rocking clothespin by pulling on the rubber band that is connected to the nail and the clothespin. The harder you pull, the slower the clothespin will rock. If you pull too hard, the clothespin will stop moving altogether.

YOU CAN CHANGE THE SPEED BY PULLING ON THE RUBBER BAND.

### Experiments to Try

You can use the wave generator and repeat the experiments you did with your finger on pages 18–19. See what results you get now.

- Position the wave generator on the edge of the test tank or on a piece of wood alongside the tank. The wood should be thick enough to allow the clothspin to clear the edge of the tank and the cork to sit just below the surface of the water. Insert the washer in any of the 4 positions. Look for wave patterns on the paper. Move the washer to the other positions and see how this affects the wave pattern.
- Move the edge of the cork close to the surface of the water or position it only slightly below it. Then repeat the above experiment. How does the depth of the cork affect the wave pattern?

- Move more and more of the metal strip holding the cork out from between the clamp end of the clothespin. What happens to the wave pattern?
- Remove the cork and tape a Popsicle stick across the metal strip. The Popsicle stick should be just below the surface of the water. Turn on the wave generator with the washer in position 1. What do you see?
- Experiment with the Popsicle stick as you did with the cork.

## What's Happening?

Whether you use finger power or motor power, the overall pattern of the waves is the same. The shape and size of the cork are close to the shape and size of your finger. As you saw previously, small round objects produce circular waves, so the cork produces circular waves. The Popsicle stick is long and straight, so it will create line waves when attached to the clothespin.

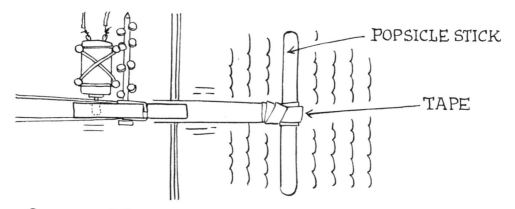

One major difference between the two situations is that the cork is bobbing up and down in the water much faster than you can move your finger. It is also making a smaller disturbance compared to what you make with your finger, because it moves only a short distance. This results in waves that are more closely spaced and smaller in size. Therefore, they will tend to die out more quickly than those made by your finger. This also holds true for the Popsicle stick attached to the clothespin.

Another difference is the size of the wave area. Earlier you saw that waves become smaller in height as they spread out, because the energy is being spread over a larger area. Since the waves made by the wave generator are already smaller, they start off with less energy. So the up-and-down movement of the water will disappear sooner compared to the waves made with your finger or the ruler.

When the bottom of the cork is just above the surface, it not only makes waves but also causes splashing. This splashing results in an irregular pattern of waves. (This also occurs when you move the metal strip farther out from the clamp end of the clothespin.) A more regular pattern appears when the bottom of the cork is just below the surface of the water.

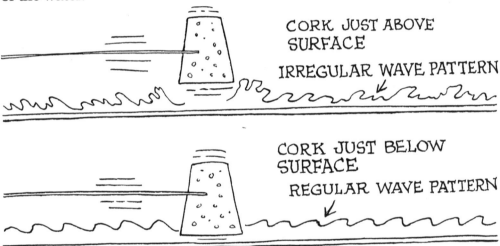

CORK JUST ABOVE SURFACE

IRREGULAR WAVE PATTERN

CORK JUST BELOW SURFACE

REGULAR WAVE PATTERN

What you see when you look at waves is energy moving through the water. After experimenting with finger power and motor power, you can draw some conclusions about how this happens. It's a gradual process, not a sudden one. The way energy is put into the water affects the size, strength, and regularity of the waves. The more energy the water receives, the longer it takes to calm down again.

Even when the waves stop, though, the energy has not vanished. Some of it is still in the water, causing slight movements. And the rest of it becomes a different kind of energy—heat.

# WAVES IN BIG SOAP FILMS

In previous sections, you made waves in a transparent container partially filled with water. What if the water were even shallower, and stretched out evenly over a much bigger area? Would the waves be the same?

In this section, you will use loops of string and soapy water to see how waves behave in a thin, wide material that moves freely in the air. Adding soap allows the water to form a film that is very thin but strong enough to wave without breaking.

This is a good activity for you and a friend because you will be experimenting with some very big loops of string.

You will need:

> 1 spool of kite string
>
> large, shallow container, like an oven roasting pan or a cat litter tray
>
> Joy or Dawn dishwashing liquid (Important: Only the most expensive dishwashing liquids work well for making very large soap-film sheets.)
>
> measuring containers, 1-cup and 1-gallon sizes
>
> wooden spoon
>
> newspaper
>
> slide projector

Step 1. Make sure the tray is thoroughly clean. Sometimes traces of substances on the tray can interfere with making a good solution with the soap. Pour about a cup of dishwashing liquid into the tray, then add about a gallon of hot water. Stir thoroughly and let the solution sit a few minutes so it can cool.

Step 2. Cut a piece of kite string 8 feet long and tie the ends together. This makes a big enough loop for 2 people to use.

Step 3.   Spread newspaper on the floor to catch any drips of soap solution.

# GETTING STARTED

Step 1.   To lift a soap film onto the string loop, you and your partner should face each other from opposite sides of the tray. Put the string loop into the soapy water so it gets wet. A soap film breaks if it touches anything dry. *Make sure the string and your hands are wet.*

Step 2.   Working slowly, you and your partner should hold the string with both hands and pull the loop out of the soap solution.

Then open up the loop by moving away from each other and spreading your hands apart. Keep moving until the sheet of soap film is horizontal.

**Step 3.** Gently shake the sheet to make waves.

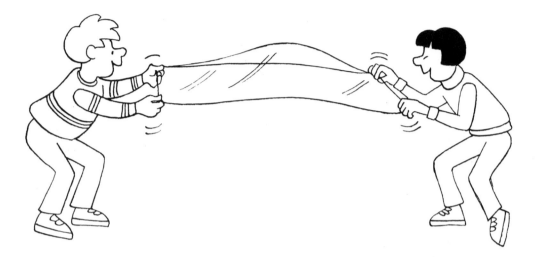

**Step 4.** Practice this technique a few times, so you and your partner can make soap films that do not break when they are held horizontally. This requires patience. You won't be able to make a soap film every time, and some of the soap films will break when you move them. Keep trying!

**Experiments to Try**

You and your partner should hold your hands about 18 inches apart. The string loop will form a soap film that is fairly big.

• Can you make a wave by gently moving an end of the string loop up and down while your partner holds the other end still?

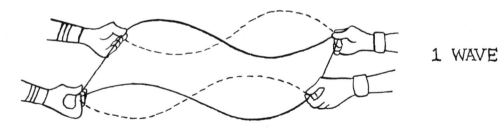

1 WAVE

• By moving one end of the string loop up and down, can you make 2, 3, 4, or 5 waves at once? Vary both the rhythm of the movement and the distance you move the end up and down.

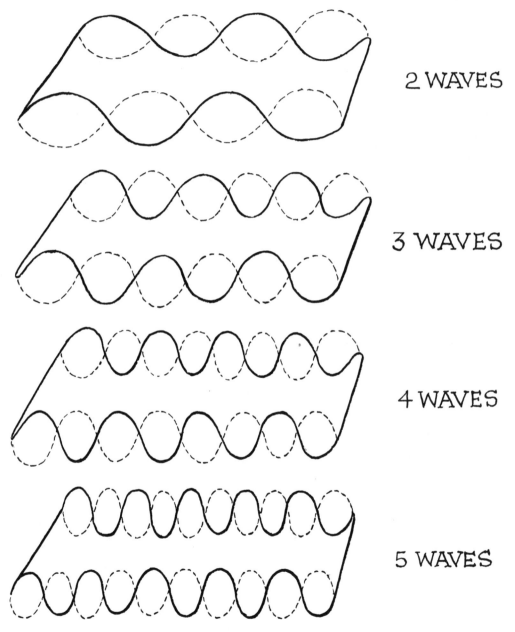

2 WAVES

3 WAVES

4 WAVES

5 WAVES

Now you and your partner can hold your hands about 10 inches apart. The string loop forms a narrow rectangle.

- Can you shake an end of the loop and get the entire sheet of soap film to move in a pattern of waves?
- What is the greatest number of waves you can make with this narrow rectangle of soap film?

Cut a piece of kite string 16 feet long and tie the ends.

- Using the same techniques and placing your and your partner's hands 18 inches apart, can you make more waves than before?
- Form this larger loop into a narrow rectangle, with your and your partner's hands 10 inches apart. Move an end up and down quickly, and then stop so that a wave is generated. Does the wave travel to the opposite end and return to the person who made it?

Hold an end of the large loop with a finger while your partner's hands are 10 inches apart. This will form a triangle.

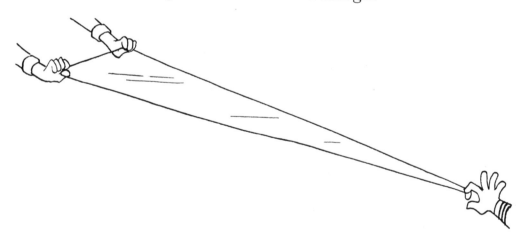

- What kind of wave pattern occurs when all sides of a triangular arrangement are shaken?

Try making a string loop using 30 feet of kite string. This time have several of your friends hold the loop to form a big circle. If all of you are very careful as you pull the string out of the soap solution and shake the soap film gently, you can make a very large undulating sheet of soap film.

You can see the shadows cast by this big soap film with the help of a slide projector. Darken the room and position the projector so that the light shines onto a blank wall. Put the tray between the wall and the projector. Make a sheet of soap film, hold it horizontally, and wave it gently while watching the shadow on the wall.

You will see an outline of the waves, and sometimes there will be flashes of bright color reflecting off the surface of the film.

• What shadow do you see when you wave the soap quickly? Slowly?

## What's Happening?

You change the number and size of waves in the soap film by changing how fast and how far you move the string loop. Moving an end slowly up and down a few feet can produce 1 to 5 big waves. Moving an end quickly up and down a few inches will result in many smaller waves. As you move your hands closer together, you have a longer, narrower sheet of soap film, and you can generate more waves. Even when only a narrow gap is left between the parallel strings, the soap film will wave.

If you quickly move an end of a sheet of soap film and stop, the resulting wave will travel to the other end and then return to its starting point. This happens slowly and the return may be weak, but you can see it if you watch very closely.

With bigger loops of string, the faster you move the ends, the smaller the waves and the more of them there will be. Very large surfaces of soap film can be made to look like the surface of the ocean. In addition, you may notice that the middle of very large soap films tends to sink where the soap solution collects. Sometimes you can see soap solution drip from the center of the soap film.

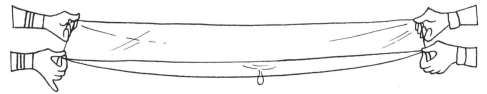

Waves made with a triangular loop start out large at the wide end but become smaller in size and closer together at the narrow end.

If you project a bright light on the soap film, you see a shadow of the waves. If you move the string loop slowly, you see a few big waves. If you move the string loop faster, you see smaller waves and more of them. This wave shadow is like a two-dimensional picture of a three-dimensional wave. It is what you would see if you could instantly freeze an ocean wave and slice through it.

This wave outline is one you will observe in many of the activities that follow in this book, and it depends on how quickly the soap film is shaken and how far up and down it is moved. A generalized wave would look like this.

Just as the waves in a small tank are like ocean waves, waves in soap film are like waves in a body of water, too. But there is a big difference: Soap-film waves disappear much more quickly than waves in a bigger body of water. Why?

One reason is that the soap film's large surface area has to fight against the air. The fact that air has resistance even when it isn't moving may surprise you. Think of a person descending to the ground in a parachute. The parachute's large open surface area takes advantage of air resistance to slow the jumper's fall. If the air did not offer resistance, the parachute would crash to the ground at full speed. As the soap film moves up and down, it fights against the air. This causes it to lose the energy that originally made it move.

Another factor is the weight of the soap film. It is so light that very little energy is needed to make it move. This small amount of energy is used up very quickly, and the waves disappear. But a big body of water is very heavy. (Just try lifting a full bucket of water and you'll see.) It takes a big blast of energy to make a big body of water move, and it is a long time before the water is calm again.

If you stand knee-deep in the surf, you may be knocked over by the force of ocean waves rolling to the shore. But if you could stand in the middle of the soap film, you would barely notice the waves as they pass you. So, in general, the heavier a material is, the more energy is needed to start a wave and to stop it.

# WAVES IN SMALL SOAP FILMS

In the last section, the big sheet of soap film allowed you to make big waves. Making small waves was harder because it was awkward to move the string loop rapidly enough. However, a smaller soap film is easier to manipulate, and it will let you see how smaller waves move on soap film.

This section will help you see if small soap films wave like big ones. You will also be looking at the differences between a flexible string loop and a more rigid wire frame. The wave generator is used to vibrate these frames. The results are fun and pleasing to watch and reveal more about the relationship between the frame's edges and the wave patterns that are created.

You will need:

        2 wire coat hangers
        1 macramé wire loop, at least 10 inches in diameter (This is
            available in a crafts shop.)
        1 cookie sheet, at least 12 inches wide, or cat litter box
        soap solution (See page 38 for directions.)
        slide projector or flashlight
        cardboard box, at least 14 inches long
        string
        ruler
        masking tape
        2 tables
        wave generator (See pages 28–33 for assembly directions.)

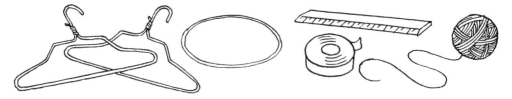

46

Step 1. Reshape a wire coat hanger so that it is as close as possible to a square.

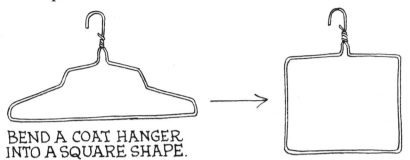

BEND A COAT HANGER
INTO A SQUARE SHAPE.

Step 2. Use the second coat hanger as is, for a triangular shape. Use the macramé loop for a circle shape.

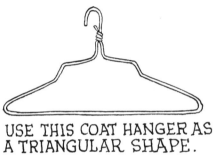

USE THIS COAT HANGER AS
A TRIANGULAR SHAPE.

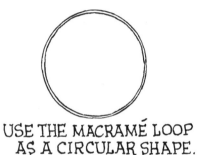

USE THE MACRAMÉ LOOP
AS A CIRCULAR SHAPE.

*Make sure the shapes are flat.* When you lay the frames on a table, all parts of the shapes should touch the table.

Step 3. Tie two 6-inch pieces of string on each frame as shown.

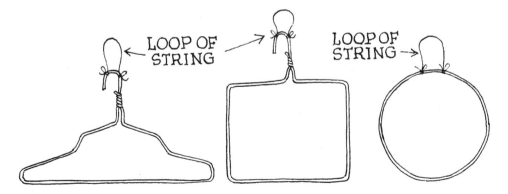

LOOP OF
STRING

LOOP OF
STRING →

Step 4.   Make a soap solution. Pour it into a wide tray.

# GETTING STARTED

Step 1.   Practice placing each frame in the soap solution and
          removing it so that a sheet of soap film is enclosed in the
          frame. The best way to do this is to pull the frame out at an
          angle and gradually move it to a vertical position. Remember
          that soap film will break immediately if it touches anything
          dry, so make sure your hands and the loops of wire are wet
          before you start.

Step 2.   Put the cardboard box upside down near the edge of a table,
          about 12 inches from a blank wall. Tape a ruler to the top of
          the box so it extends a few inches out, like a diving board. Put
          the projector or flashlight on another table and aim the light
          at the box. Darken the room.

Step 3.   Using the string loops, hang a framed soap film from the
          ruler. Adjust the position of the cardboard box or the light so
          you see a good reflection of the soap film on the blank wall.

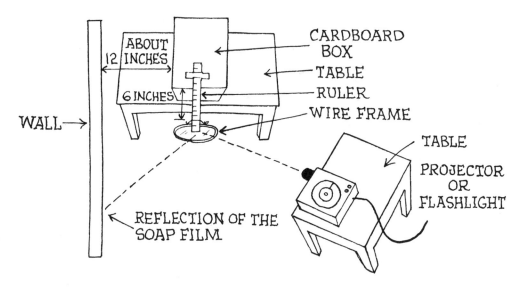

## Experiments to Try

Select a frame, make a soap film, and hang the frame on the ruler. Wait until the frame stops moving.

• Tap the cardboard box with your finger. Try tapping lightly with a steady rhythm, and then tap harder. Try a fast rhythm, then a slow one. Watch the reflection on the wall. How does your tapping change the reflection?

Repeat these experiments with the other shapes.

• How does the shape of the frame affect the shape of the waves?
• How do the waves in these small soap films compare to the waves in the big soap films?

Another way to make a soap-film wave is with the wave generator.

You will have to position the generator by trial and error. The way the vibrations travel through the cardboard box and the ruler will depend on what type of box and ruler you use.

Touch the ruler lightly with the vibrating cork of the generator. (If the ruler vibrates too much, the reflection will be blurred.) You will have to experiment with the washer position (see pages 34–35). You should also test parts of the ruler and box to see which give the best results.

• Experiment with different ways of touching the cardboard box or ruler with the vibrating cork or the wood base of the generator. Which way produces the most interesting patterns?
• Try varying the speed of the wave generator's motor. How does this affect the wave patterns?
• Try making frames in other shapes and using them to make soap films. What wave patterns do you see? Throughout the experiments, remember to make drawings of each pattern you observe.

49

## What's Happening?

When the soap film is not disturbed by vibrations, the reflection shows large bands of color. When the frame is tapped, there are dark and bright lines that form a definite pattern.

Soap film is very sensitive to any kind of disturbance, so the slightest vibration will show up in the reflection on the wall. When you tap on the cardboard box with your finger, a disturbance travels from the cardboard box along the ruler and string loop to the frame. The frame vibrates, which in turn moves the soap film. Tapping on the cardboard box tends to make fewer, more widely spaced circles. The wave generator's faster motion produces thinner and more closely spaced circles.

If you carefully observe the patterns produced in the square frame, you can see something like a checkerboard design. Round frames, in contrast, produce circular waves.

The pattern produced in the triangular frame is more complex and is harder to see. You should find that it looks something like a pattern of diamonds.

Oddly shaped frames produce complex patterns like those made in the triangular one.

The wave generator produces waves similar to the ones made by tapping a finger, but they are smaller, whether the frame is circular, square, or triangular.

As you go from a fast speed to a slower speed with the wave generator, the resulting vibrating pattern becomes simpler and the elements of the overall pattern grow larger.

If you compare the patterns produced in this activity to your drawings of the waves in the tank, they will look similar. This is not accidental. Even though the sizes of the waves are different, the shapes are the same. By adjusting the amount of energy you use and the rate at which you disturb the water or soap film, you can always make similar patterns of waves.

# WAVES ON CURVES

So far, you've been experimenting with water and soap film, which
have a flat surface when they are at rest. What do waves look like on a
curved surface, for instance, a raindrop? Raindrops are curved, and
they shake and wiggle as they fall. If you could take photographs of
them, the patterns of movement would look like waves. But raindrops
are hard to experiment with.

In this section, you will use a large soap-film bubble dome to see
how waves move along a curve. (A *bubble dome* is a bubble that's
resting on a surface rather than floating free in the air.)

You will need:
> 1 disposable plastic plate, 9 inches in diameter
> 1 disposable plastic plate, 12 inches in diameter
> 1 metal pizza pan
> 1 piece of cardboard, about 24 inches long and 14 inches
>    wide
> tin can open at both ends
> soap solution (See page 38 for directions.)
> slide projector or overhead light without dowels (See pages
>    12–14 for assembly directions.)
> 3 chairs of equal height

Step 1.  Find a place that can be made dark, the darker the better. It should be big enough for you to move around in and should have a blank wall.

Step 2.  Place 2 chairs 8 to 10 inches apart, facing each other. The chairs should be right next to a wall.

Step 3.  Position the slide projector or overhead light and battery holder on another chair so that the light shines on the blank wall.

Step 4.  Put the piece of cardboard between the 2 chairs.

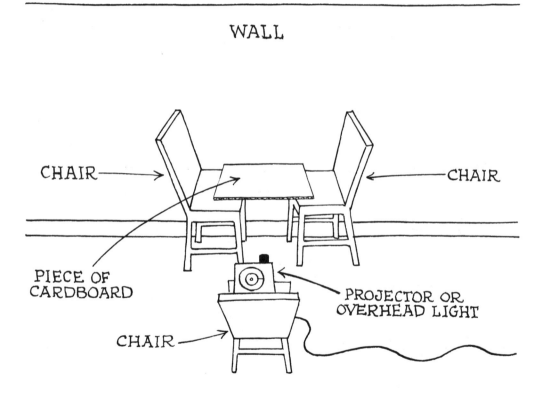

WALL

CHAIR

CHAIR

PIECE OF CARDBOARD

PROJECTOR OR OVERHEAD LIGHT

CHAIR

Place the 9-inch plastic plate in the middle of the cardboard and pour soap solution onto the plate. Remember that soap films break if they touch something dry, so make sure the sides of the plate are wet.

# MAKING BUBBLE DOMES

The bubble dome is made by blowing through the open-ended tin can. You will need some practice to make large, complete bubble domes that do not pop when you are blowing them.

Step 1.  Put an end of the tin can into the soap solution in the plate.

Step 2.  Tilt the can and pull it up at an angle, so that a window of soap film forms over the bottom end of the can.

Step 3.  Hold the can about 2 inches from the plate and blow into it with a long, steady breath. If you blow too hard, the soap film will break. If you blow too gently, a dome will not form. Experiment until you blow at the right speed and the bubble forms on the plate. Keep moving the can up as the bubble grows. Also, as it grows, keep the can just inside the dome.

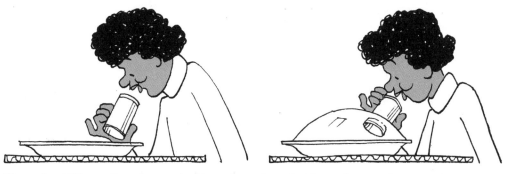

Step 4.  When the dome is 7 or 8 inches high, release the can from the dome by tilting it to the side and pulling it away. This maneuver will take some practice, too, but be patient. The results you get are beautiful and well worth the effort.

# GETTING STARTED

Once you have perfected your technique for making complete bubble domes, you can now make them wave. Since the piece of cardboard is somewhat flexible, it will vibrate the plate and the dome if you tap on it. Darken the room and adjust the projector or light so that you see a good shadow of the bubble dome on the wall. It should be a perfect semicircle of very brilliant colors.

## Experiments to Try

• Tap the cardboard lightly. Tap a little harder, but at the same speed. Tap quickly and lightly. Tap quickly with a little more force. What happens to the dome as your tapping changes?
• Blow bubble domes of different sizes. How does the shape of the waves change as you make and vibrate bigger and bigger bubble domes?
• What happens if you blow bubble domes on the larger 12-inch plastic plate or on a metal pan such as a pizza pan?
• What does the vibrating bubble dome look like when you look down at it from above?

You can also make the bubble dome vibrate by waving your hand back and forth a few inches away from the dome. This moves the air, which shakes the soap film. You will need practice to find the right distance between your hand and the dome so the bubble vibrates but does not break. Then you can experiment with the rhythm of your hand movements.

• What does the dome look like as you move your hand near it? How are these changing shapes different from the ones you made by tapping the cardboard?

## What's Happening?

Hans Jenny, a scientist who spent many years experimenting with wave patterns of different materials, studied vibrating bubble domes.

He found that the higher the dome, the greater the number of waves on the surface. The following drawings show some of his results.

If you took a picture of your vibrating bubble dome, it would be similar to these drawings. When you tap on the piece of cardboard at a slow rate and with some force, you see a few waves on the surface of the dome. Tapping faster makes more waves on the surface.

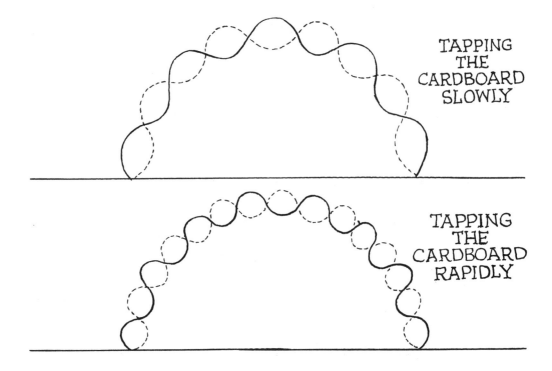

TAPPING THE CARDBOARD SLOWLY

TAPPING THE CARDBOARD RAPIDLY

Larger domes are easier to shake, but tend to break sooner.

There isn't much difference in the shape of the waves as you go from smaller to larger bubbles. However, it is easier to see the wave forms with the larger domes.

If you look down on the vibrating bubble dome, you see moving rings, with the smallest at the top. Notice that at the very top of the dome, the soap film moves in and out. At one moment, it forms a small mountain, and the next, a small depression.

Elsewhere on the bubble dome, the rings are moving in and out, too. At one moment a ring bulges out, and then it caves in, forming a depression. You can see this movement in two dimensions in the shadow on the wall. When you look at several rings, this in-and-out movement looks like, and is, a wave.

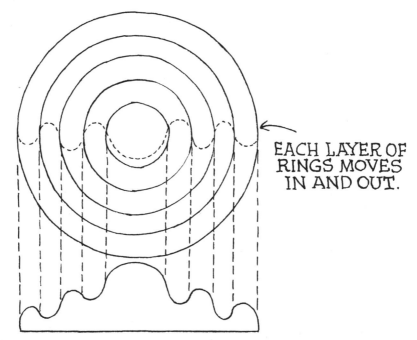

EACH LAYER OF RINGS MOVES IN AND OUT.

Moving your hand near the bubble causes a section of the dome's surface to move in and out. The overall pattern is not circular now, but more irregular and lumpy. By experimenting with different hand movements and rhythms, you can cause the whole bubble dome to dance in amusing ways.

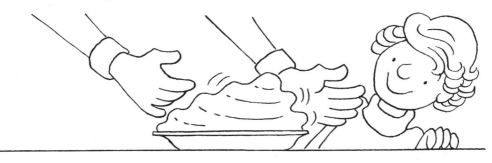

# TINY WAVES

If you compare all the drawings you made during your explorations, you will see how similar water waves are, whether they are in $\frac{1}{2}$ inch of water in a tank or in a paper-thin sheet of soap film. This kind of progression from the large scale to the small is an important part of science. When scientists see something that remains the same in both large-scale and small-scale tests, they know that what they have found is true and important.

Sometimes, however, scientists find a point where the scale becomes so large or so small that the thing they are studying behaves differently.

In this section, you will experiment with tiny waves, the ones you might see when you slide a paper cup filled with water across a table. These tiny waves are different from all the other waves you have studied.

You will need:

       1 disposable plastic plate, 9 or 12 inches in diameter
       wave generator (See pages 28–33 for assembly directions.)
       blue food coloring
       water
       cup measure
       table

Step 1. Make a solution of blue water by adding a few drops of blue food coloring to about 1 cup of water. The blue color will make it easier to see the tiny waves.

Step 2. Pour the water solution into the plastic plate to just cover the bottom of the plate—no deeper. Set the plate down on a table.

Step 3. Hold the wave generator in your hand and insert the washer in position 4 to start the motor at full speed.

**Experiments to Try**

• Touch the moving end of the clothespin to the edge of the plastic plate. Because of slight variations in these plates, they vibrate differently depending on where they are touched. Therefore, move the clothespin to different parts of the plate. When you touch a sensitive spot, very small waves will appear on the water. What pattern do the waves make?

• Experiment with different amounts of pressure when you touch the wave generator to the plate. What happens to the waves when you stop touching the clothespin to the plate?

**What's Happening?**

In this activity, you see several behaviors you have not seen before. First, the wave pattern looks hexagonal.

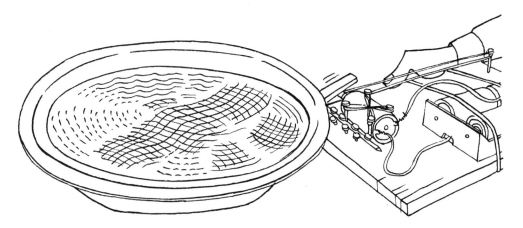

Second, when you stop touching the clothespin to the plate, the waves stop immediately.

Other waves you have explored are patterns of lines and circles. They run deeper than these tiny waves, stir up much more water, and keep moving even after the disturbance stops. Even the waves in the soap film—the thinnest material you have worked with—follow these rules.

But the tiny waves do not. A small amount of energy, moving from the plastic plate to the water, disturbs only the very top surface of the water.

Larger waves, such as those found in the ocean, a lake, a swimming pool, or even your bathtub, act differently. In these places, both the surface and some of the water below it are disturbed. A large amount of effort had to be made to start these waves. With tiny waves, however, only a very thin surface layer of water is disturbed by a small amount of energy.

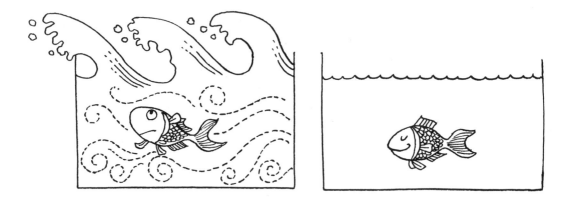

These experiments show that the amount of pressure can make a difference in whether waves form or not. Different amounts of pressure may or may not result in patterns forming.

# WAVES IN SOLIDS

How are waves in solids like waves in liquids?

The following activities will help you explore the wave motions of some familiar solids: sheets of thin plastic, lengths of rope, and lengths of string and elastic.

## WAVING SHEETS

In a previous investigation, you explored waving sheets of soap film. Because soap film is so thin, the waves move easily from one end of a loop of string to the other.

Plastic drop cloths are also very thin but are thicker than soap film. They are also less flexible. These sheets come in several different thicknesses. Therefore, you can experiment with the relationship between thickness and the amount of energy needed to make waves.

This kind of investigation can be taken a step further by playing around with bed sheets or blankets. Look around your house to see what you have available. You'll need to work with at least 3 or 4 other people so that you can stretch the materials out flat before and while you do the experiments.

You will need:
  plastic drop cloths, in 1-mil, 3-mil, and other thicknesses
    (These are available at hardware or paint stores.)
  bed sheets
  large blankets

**Experiments to Try**

This activity involves at least 4 people, with each person holding a side of a plastic drop cloth.

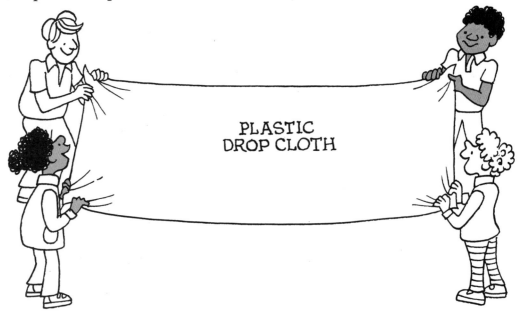

For all of the following experiments, move the drop cloth with big, slow movements, then with small, fast ones.

- With 1 person at each corner, take turns moving 1 corner up and down. What are the waves like?
- Try having 2 people at a time move the sheet simultaneously. First, 2 people on the same side can move their end up and down. Second, 2 people on opposite sides can move their ends. What are the resulting wave patterns?
- What happens if 2 people on the same side of the plastic sheet move their corners up and down a few feet just once and stop?
- Now try all of these experiments with different thicknesses of drop cloths and then with the bed sheets and the blankets. Remember to write down the similarities and differences among the different materials.

## What's Happening?

The waves you make with the various kinds of plastic and cloth materials are generally similar to those you produced with water and soap films. When a person moves the cloth, the ripples move out to the person directly across from him or her, in the same way they would travel to the opposite side in water. Two people moving the cloth in a rhythmic manner can produce lines of ripples moving around the cloth. When everyone moves the sheet of cloth up and down together, there is no wave across the cloth. The whole piece forms a big bulge when the cloth moves up and also when it moves down. When all 4 people move the cloth at different times, the surface becomes chaotic. It looks similar to the waves on the ocean or a lake on a windy day.

When a short disturbance is made at an end and allowed to travel outward, a very faint ripple will move to the opposite end and return to the sender.

Different kinds of materials will generally act in similar ways. If you use a heavy blanket, it will take more effort to make the whole blanket ripple than it did a very thin drop cloth. Stiffer drop cloths also seem to require a little more effort both to make waves and to keep them moving.

There are several observations you can make about wave movement in solid materials. Heavier things require more energy to disturb their surface than lighter things. Heavier things like blankets also require a lot of energy and a continuous disturbance to keep the waves appearing, because of the weight as well as the friction in the material. The many fibers in the wool or cloth rub against one another, using up the energy very quickly.

This does not happen to plastic sheets. Since the sheet has no fibers and tends to stretch a little when it is disturbed, the waves travel more easily and quickly along it.

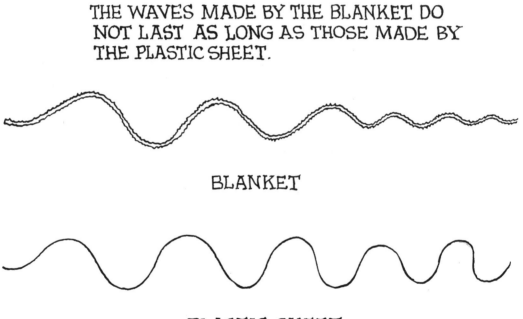

THE WAVES MADE BY THE BLANKET DO NOT LAST AS LONG AS THOSE MADE BY THE PLASTIC SHEET.

BLANKET

PLASTIC SHEET

At this point, it is difficult to say how much the weight and flexibility affect the wave movement. In the last section of this book, you will investigate these factors in a more controlled manner.

# WAVING LINES

In the previous activity, you made the waves move up and down with the movement of your hands. But you also saw that they move across the bed sheet, so that the whole sheet waves. This makes it hard to see how a single wave moves.

When you make a rope or a length of string wave, the waves go only in two directions: up and down or side to side. However, the waves in the waving line are similar to those in the waving bed sheet. It is as if you were looking only at a long thread in the waving bed sheet.

BED SHEET

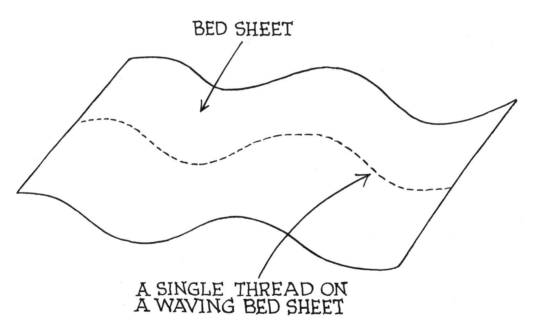

A SINGLE THREAD ON
A WAVING BED SHEET

If you have a long clothesline hanging near your house, or if you have played jump rope, you may already have tried to make waves with a rope. You can make very big waves or lots of little ones with this material. By experimenting with other kinds of materials, you can also investigate how properties such as weight, elasticity, and flexibility affect the generation and movement of waves.

You will need:

> 1 piece of clothesline rope, at least 16 feet long (the longer the better)
>
> 1 piece of kite string, 10 feet long
>
> 1 piece of heavy twine for wrapping packages, 10 feet long
>
> 1 piece of gauge 22 or 26 electrical wire, 10 feet long
>
> 1 piece of elastic thread, 10 feet long (This is available in the sewing-supplies section of most department stores. This thread comes in several widths; buy at least 2 widths so you can make comparisons between them.)
>
> 1 piece of metal strapping or flexible metal, 10 feet long (This is often found lying around lumberyards. It is used to hold bundles of wood planks together. Ask at a lumberyard for scrap pieces.) (optional)
>
> a Slinky (optional)

**Experiments to Try**

You can do these explorations by yourself. But it is easier and more fun to experiment with a friend. Each of you can hold an end of the material to see how many different ways you can make waves.

- What is the highest number of waves you can make with each material?
- Can you and your friend move your hands in a rhythm that makes 1 big wave?

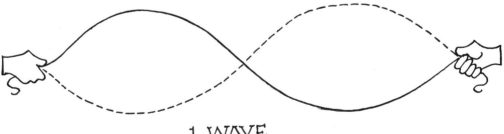

1 WAVE

• Can you find rhythms that make 2, 3, 4, 5, and 6 waves?

2 WAVES

3 WAVES

4 WAVES

5 WAVES

6 WAVES

- What happens if you lay the material on a bare floor and try making sideways waves that slide along the floor?
- If a person gives a quick jerk to the material, does the resulting wave travel to the opposite end and then back to its starting point?

**What's Happening?**

You can shake all of the materials to make a waving motion. The greater the distance that you move your arms up and down, the more waves you make.

When you shake some of the materials, such as the clothesline rope and the Slinky, they give a good picture of how they are waving. You can see individual sections alternate between rising and falling. The kite string, elastic thread, and twine have to be shaken faster to keep the waves from disappearing quickly. The electrical wire bends too easily, so it is difficult to make it wave. On the other hand, when you shake a piece of metal strapping in a rhythmic manner, it is easy to generate waves.

You can also get a single wave to travel from one end of the waving line to the other. And shaking these materials while they are lying on the floor gives you an especially good picture of how the waves are forming.

In all the other investigations, surfaces were disturbed and wave movement was observed. Here you disturb only a thin line of material and see that it generally acts in a similar way. Also, some materials seem to be easier to wave than others. With both surfaces and lines, factors such as relative heaviness and the flexibility of the materials seem to be important. However, it is difficult to tell from this kind of experimentation how important each factor is in making a wave. A more systematic approach has to be taken, and only one element at a time must be changed. You will examine these more closely in later investigations.

# STANDING WAVES

If you could shake the end of the piece of kite string or the thin elastic thread fast enough, you might be able to make waves travel along them. To do this, you would need something that moves back and forth very quickly: the wave generator. You can observe beautiful patterns as you make the motor rotate at different speeds. You may be surprised at the results!

You will need:

      1 piece of elastic thread, 10 feet long
      1 piece of kite string, 10 feet long
      1 piece of kite string, 20 feet long
      1 piece of kite string, 5 feet long
      1 piece of clothesline rope, 16 feet long
      1 piece of gauge 22 or 26 electrical wire, 10 feet long
      wave generator (See pages 28–33 for assembly directions.)
      10 plastic drinking straws
      2 chairs

Step 1.    Place 2 chairs about 9 feet apart, facing each other.
Step 2.    Put the wave generator and battery holder on a chair.
Step 3.    Tie an end of the 10-foot length of kite string to a leg of the other chair.

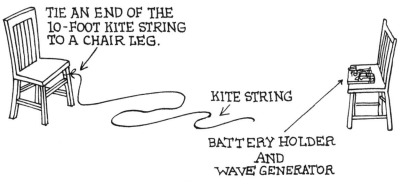

TIE AN END OF THE 10-FOOT KITE STRING TO A CHAIR LEG.

KITE STRING

BATTERY HOLDER AND WAVE GENERATOR

Step 4.  Tie the other end of the kite string to the clothespin on the
        wave generator.

TIE THE END OF THE KITE STRING
SECURELY TO THIS END OF ⟶
THE CLOTHESPIN.

Step 5.  Pull the chairs apart so the string stretches straight but is not
        too tight.

# GETTING STARTED

Start the motor of the wave generator by inserting the washer in
position 1. (See pages 34–35 for directions.) You should see the string
vibrating. Vary the tightness of the string by moving the chairs farther
apart or closer together. Keep working on the tension until you get a
wave that seems to move up and down, but not across. It should look
as if it is running in place.

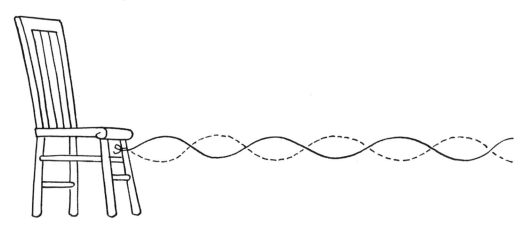

**Experiments to Try**
• Use positions 2, 3, and 4 on the wave generator. How do the different
  speeds affect the wave pattern?

- What happens if you move the wave generator forward or backward slightly (less than 1 inch)? How does changing the tension on the kite string affect the waves produced?
- Try using the 10-foot length of elastic thread and then the 20-foot length of kite string. How do these wave patterns compare to the waves in the 10-foot length of kite string?
- Disconnect the end of the 20-foot length of kite string from the wave generator and tie it to the chair leg. Move the wave generator to the floor. Tie an end of the 5-foot length of kite string to the midpoint of the 20-foot length of kite string and the other end to the wave generator.

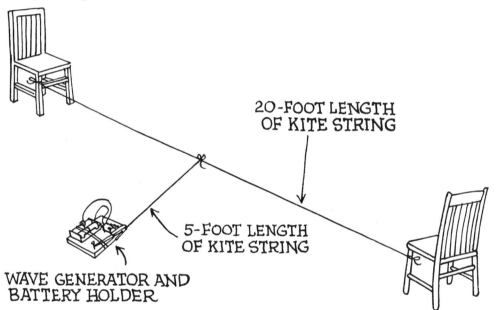

20-FOOT LENGTH OF KITE STRING

5-FOOT LENGTH OF KITE STRING

WAVE GENERATOR AND BATTERY HOLDER

Does the 5-foot length of kite string vibrate when the wave generator is turned on?
- Now see if you can make the piece of clothesline rope or the electrical wire wave with the wave generator. Leave the wave generator on the floor. Attach an end of the rope or wire to the clothespin and tie the other end to one of the chairs. Can the wave generator make the material wave in position 4?

- Make a chain of straws by squeezing the end of a straw and inserting it into another straw. Put all 10 straws together in this way.

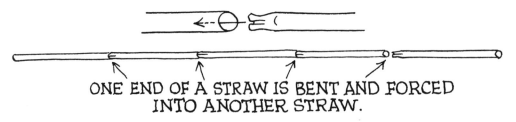

ONE END OF A STRAW IS BENT AND FORCED
INTO ANOTHER STRAW.

Attach an end of the chain of straws to the wave generator. (It should still be on the floor.) Let the other end of the chain hang free. How does the chain of straws move when the clothespin vibrates?

**What's Happening?**
You should have seen that the clothespin moves up and down fast enough to cause the kite string to vibrate along its entire length. Changing the speed of the motor, the tension on the kite string, or the length of string will change the number and size of waves that appear on the string. Elastic thread behaves in a very similar way. A chain of plastic straws can also be made to vibrate because they are lightweight and flexible.

But heavier materials like clothesline rope do not wave because the wave generator isn't strong enough to move them. The electrical wire may or may not vibrate, depending on how heavy and flexible it is.

When an extra piece of string is attached to the midpoint of the 20-foot piece of string, a waving motion still occurs. Both the longer string and the new addition will shake.

These experiments give you a clear picture of some important properties of waves. Waving materials usually look as if they are in constant motion. By using the wave generator and adjusting the tension and length of the material you are using, you can make a wave that seems to run in place. It moves up and down but not outward

72

along the length of the line. It looks like a series of seesaws. It is called a *standing wave*.

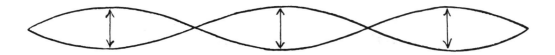

The standing wave is important because it shows you something that is true of every wave in every material. There are points of maximum movement, called *antinodes*, where the wave pattern is at its highest and lowest. And there is a point of no movement at all, called the *node*, at the spot where the highs and lows meet.

A WAVE LOOKS LIKE THIS AT ONE MOMENT...

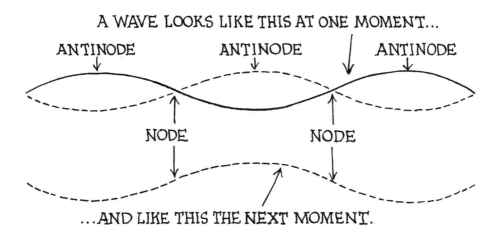

...AND LIKE THIS THE NEXT MOMENT.

In a standing wave, you can see this clearly because the wave pattern is "on hold"—it is without all the confusing movement you usually see in waves. You can see individual sections of the waves and see how much or how little they move. In the next chapter, you will use wave models, made out of dowels and tape and other materials, to look further at basic wave movement.

# MODEL WAVE MACHINES

If you look back over the activities you've done so far, you can see a progression from fairly big surfaces and lots of waves to much smaller surfaces and fewer waves. In the last activity, you made a standing wave, which is the simplest wave you can produce in an everyday material.

But even a kite string caught in a standing wave is going too fast for careful study. Model wave machines are the next step. They wave so slowly and so simply that you can see a wave moving at a crawl. And they make it easy to see the effects of the different changes you make.

## WAVE MACHINE #1: A CENTIPEDE

In the nineteenth century a scientist named James Clerk Maxwell made a model wave machine with metal bars and metal strapping in order to investigate some properties of waves. When he measured how far and how often the bars swung in different experiments, and how long they stayed in motion, he found a clear mathematical relationship. When he discovered this relationship, he could use mathematics to predict accurately how the bars would move in an experiment.

This was a critical breakthrough in the study of waves. When scientists can predict how a phenomenon will behave under different conditions, then they really understand it.

In the next series of activities you will make versions of Maxwell's model wave machine using dowels and tape and nails. These machines

74

will help you see and understand waves better, and they are also fun to watch. When you finish your experiments, you can keep them as *kinetic*, or moving, sculptures.

The first wave machine you make is the biggest. It looks like a giant centipede, with a spine of tape and legs made of wooden dowels.

You will need:
> 40 dowels, 12 inches long and $\frac{1}{8}$ inch in diameter
> 1 dowel, 24 inches long and $\frac{1}{8}$ inch in diameter
> 1 roll of masking tape, $\frac{1}{2}$ inch wide
> about 6 pounds of nails (350 to 360 nails), 3 inches long
> ruler
> rubber bands
> 2 chairs or tables of equal height

Step 1.  Find a table or clear an area on the floor that is at least 8 feet long and 2 or 3 feet wide. Carefully lay a 10-foot-long piece of $\frac{1}{2}$-inch masking tape, sticky side up, on this surface. Anchor the piece of masking tape to the floor by putting two 4- or 5-inch pieces of masking tape about 10 inches in from each end of the strip.

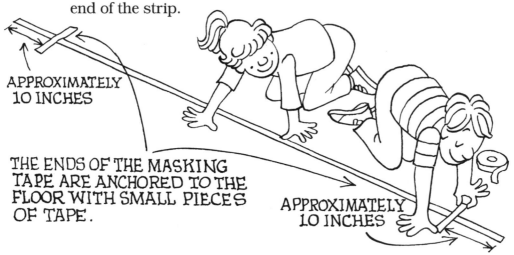

APPROXIMATELY 10 INCHES

THE ENDS OF THE MASKING TAPE ARE ANCHORED TO THE FLOOR WITH SMALL PIECES OF TAPE.

APPROXIMATELY 10 INCHES

Step 2.  Make a mark in the middle of each of the 12-inch dowels.

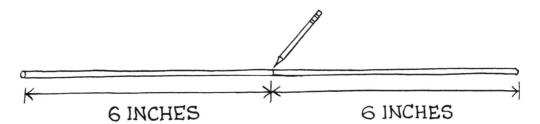

**6 INCHES**          **6 INCHES**

Step 3.  About $17\frac{1}{2}$ inches in from an end of the piece of masking tape, lay a dowel across the tape. Use the mark you made to center the dowel on the tape. Press down firmly so the dowel sticks to the tape. Place another dowel $1\frac{1}{2}$ inches from the first one. Center it and press down firmly. Continue to add dowels until you reach the anchor tape at the other end. When you finish, all the dowels should be between the 2 anchor tapes.

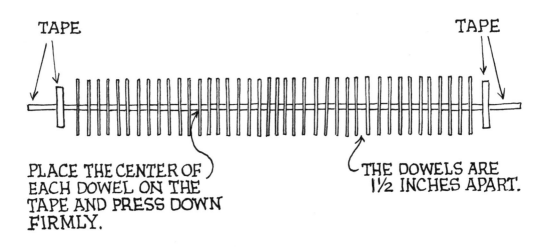

TAPE                                        TAPE

PLACE THE CENTER OF EACH DOWEL ON THE TAPE AND PRESS DOWN FIRMLY.

THE DOWELS ARE 1½ INCHES APART.

Step 4.  Carefully place another strip of $\frac{1}{2}$-inch masking tape on an end dowel. Press the tape around the dowel, over the strip of tape beneath the dowel, and around the next dowel. Keep working slowly until you reach the other end dowel.

Step 5.   Secure four 3-inch nails to both ends of every dowel with a rubber band. (The nails add weight.)

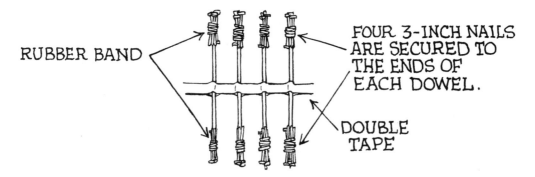

RUBBER BAND

FOUR 3-INCH NAILS ARE SECURED TO THE ENDS OF EACH DOWEL.

DOUBLE TAPE

Step 6.   Carefully lift the wave machine and suspend it between the backs of 2 chairs or the edges of 2 tables. Secure the ends of the wave machine to the chairs or tables with masking tape. Pull the chairs or tables apart enough so that there is no slack in the wave machine. But do not pull it too tight.

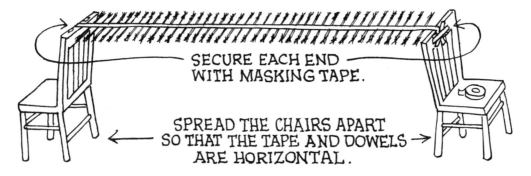

SECURE EACH END WITH MASKING TAPE.

SPREAD THE CHAIRS APART SO THAT THE TAPE AND DOWELS ARE HORIZONTAL.

**Experiments to Try**

Before you do each of these experiments, make sure you give the dowels time to come to a complete stop.

• Push different dowels, one at a time, to see what happens. Try fast and slow movements, then continuous and stop-and-start movements. Each time, note how long it takes for the wave to travel to both ends of the machine, and also note changes in the overall pattern of wave movement.

- Move one of the middle dowels, wait about 5 seconds, and move the same dowel in the same way again. What happens as the 2 energy pulses reach the farthest dowel? When the 2 waves approach each other, do they combine or do they pass each other unchanged?
- What does the whole device look like when you move a dowel back and forth repeatedly for 1 minute or more?
- What happens if you give an end dowel a big push?
- What happens if you move an end dowel while firmly holding one of the middle dowels? Does the movement stop at the dowel you are holding, or does it move beyond it? What happens if you hold the dowel very loosely?
- Separate the chairs or tables enough to make the tape as tight as possible without breaking or pulling away. Move any dowel back and forth rhythmically. How does the movement change when there is more tension on the tape?
- Secure 20 nails to each end of the 24-inch dowel. Remove the nails from both ends of one of the middle dowels of the wave machine. Attach the 24-inch dowel to this one with rubber bands.

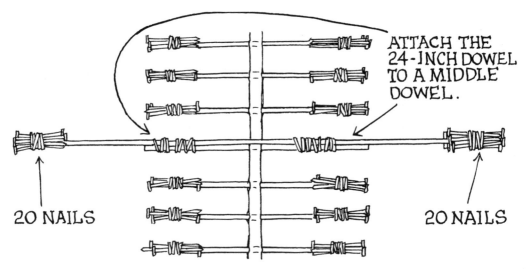

ATTACH THE 24-INCH DOWEL TO A MIDDLE DOWEL.

20 NAILS

20 NAILS

Move an end dowel and watch carefully as the movement travels along the tape. What happens when it reaches this long dowel?

- Remove 10 nails from each end of the long dowel and repeat the experiment. What happens?
- Replace the long dowel with a 12-inch dowel. Then remove all the nails from both ends of 4 dowels (2 on either side of it). The other 35 dowels should still have 4 nails at each end. Move an end dowel. Watch carefully as the movement travels along the tape. What happens when it reaches the unweighted dowels?

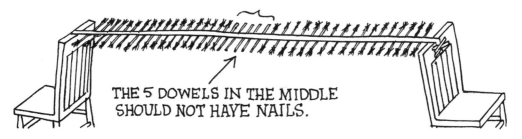

THE 5 DOWELS IN THE MIDDLE SHOULD NOT HAVE NAILS.

- Remove 3 nails from each end of every dowel. How does this affect the movement of the wave? What happens if you put a total of 10 nails on each end of 1 dowel?

**What's Happening?**

Whenever you disturb a dowel or a group of them, movement travels along the tape and out to both ends of the device. If you watch from the side of the device, you'll see the dowels make a wavelike pattern similar to the ones you observed in the waving water, soap film, bed sheets, and lines.

When you move a dowel back and forth rhythmically at a certain rate, some dowels move a lot and others don't move at all. This pattern is similar to a standing wave.

Whether you give a big or gentle push to a dowel, the resulting movement will look the same. However, a bigger initial push will result in the traveling wave lasting longer, and it will be easier to see that the pulse of energy is reflected off the end of the device. This action is similar to what occurs when a wave is reflected off the side of a swimming pool or when the end of a long rope has been snapped quickly. The end of the strip of masking tape becomes twisted by the pulse of energy and then immediately untwists itself. Some energy is lost in this twisting back and forth, so a weaker pulse is sent back down the strip of tape.

When both pulses of energy meet each other, they will pass and continue in the same direction in which they have been going. You may not be able to see this at first, especially if the pulses are of equal energy. To see this passing action more clearly, send a strong pulse of energy by giving an end dowel a big push, then wait a few seconds and send a weaker pulse along the masking tape. Watch carefully. When the first pulse of energy returns and meets the second one, you should see both pulses emerge, largely unchanged. One is still stronger than the other, and each is still moving in its original direction.

When you hold a dowel and push another, the pulse of energy reflects off the dowel you are holding and returns to its starting point. If you hold a dowel very loosely, some of the energy from the traveling pulse of energy may continue on through the tape to the other dowels.

Something similar happens when you attach the 24-inch dowel to a middle dowel. If there are 20 nails on this longer dowel, most of the pulse of energy will be reflected back to the starting point. Reducing the number of nails on the ends of the longer dowel increases the chance that the energy pulse will continue beyond this dowel.

In the earlier experiments with water, soap film, bed sheets, and lines, you learned about the importance of a material's weight and flexibility. In the wave machine, you control weight by adding or removing nails. When you add nails to all the dowels, the pulse of energy moves more slowly up the tape. The pulse goes faster when you remove some nails from all or some of the dowels, or when you increase the tension on the tape by pulling it taut.

## A Further Challenge

You can do more experiments with your wave machine and make other wave machines with different characteristics. For instance, you can make one just like the first but use 1-inch tape instead of $\frac{1}{2}$-inch tape. Or you can make the tape stiffer on the one you already constructed by placing another layer of tape over the existing tape.

You should find that in both of these wave machines the wave movement travels faster to each end and is reflected back more quickly.

# WAVE MACHINE #2: FOUR CONNECTED DOWELS

In this activity, you will look more closely at flexibility and weight, and at what happens when the dowels are connected to one another. Wave machine #2 is smaller than #1, so it is easier to make changes. It is also constructed a little differently to allow you to connect the dowels.

With wave machine #2, you can see how energy is transferred through wave movement between the 4 connected dowels. The resulting movement is probably not what you expect, which is part of the fun of this activity.

You will need:

> 3 yardsticks (These are available from a hardware store or in the hardware section of a department store.)
> 6 dowels, 36 inches long and $\frac{1}{8}$ inch in diameter
> paper clips
> about 60 #16 rubber bands
> 208 finishing nails, 3 inches long
> hacksaw
> masking tape
> 2 chairs or tables of equal height

# MAKING A SUPPORT STRUCTURE

Step 1.   Use the hacksaw to cut 2 dowels into eight 6-inch pieces. (You will have a long piece of dowel left over.)

Step 2.   Tape a paper clip to the middle of each 6-inch dowel. Make sure you do not tape over the opening of the paper clip.

TAPE A PAPER CLIP TO THE MIDDLE OF EACH 6-INCH DOWEL. — LEAVE A SMALL HOLE.

Step 3.   Attach the 6-inch dowels to 2 of the yardsticks. Loop the rubber bands around the dowels so that they are held tightly. The placement of each dowel is important. They should be lined up 4 inches apart, as shown in the drawing.

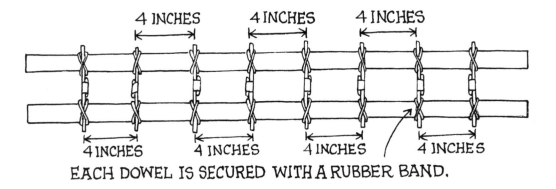

4 INCHES   4 INCHES   4 INCHES

4 INCHES   4 INCHES   4 INCHES   4 INCHES

EACH DOWEL IS SECURED WITH A RUBBER BAND.

Step 4.   Rotate the dowels so that the openings of the paper clips are midway between the 2 yardsticks and lined up with one another. Each set of 2 paper clips should face each other but hang down from the dowels.

Step 5. Hang this support structure between 2 chairs or tables and secure the ends of it with masking tape.

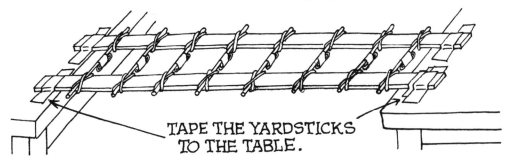

TAPE THE YARDSTICKS TO THE TABLE.

# MAKING AND HANGING THE DOWELS

Step 1. Use the hacksaw to cut four 4-inch pieces from the remaining yardstick.

Step 2. Put a 4-inch piece of yardstick on a table. Lay a 36-inch dowel over it so that the dowel extends $\frac{1}{2}$ inch beyond the edge of the piece of yardstick. Wrap a rubber band around the dowel and piece of yardstick so they are held together tightly and cannot be twisted easily.

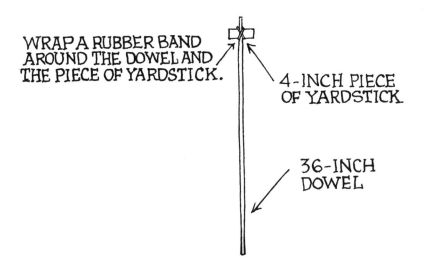

WRAP A RUBBER BAND AROUND THE DOWEL AND THE PIECE OF YARDSTICK.

4-INCH PIECE OF YARDSTICK

36-INCH DOWEL

**Step 3.** Slide the 4-inch piece of yardstick along the dowel until it is about 14 inches from the end of the dowel.

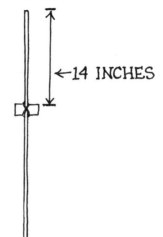

←14 INCHES

**Step 4.** Tape a nail on each side of the 4-inch piece of yardstick so the points of the nails extend about $\frac{1}{2}$ inch beyond the yardstick.

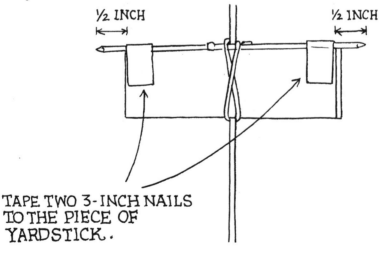

½ INCH    ½ INCH

TAPE TWO 3-INCH NAILS
TO THE PIECE OF
YARDSTICK.

**Step 5.** Follow Steps 2, 3, and 4 to make a total of 4 identical dowels.

**Step 6.** Make a "weight packet" by wrapping 20 nails with a rubber band. Make a total of 8 of these packets.

Step 7. With a rubber band, attach a weight packet to each end of the 4 dowels.

Step 8. Hang the dowels from the support structure by inserting the points of the nails through the paper clips.

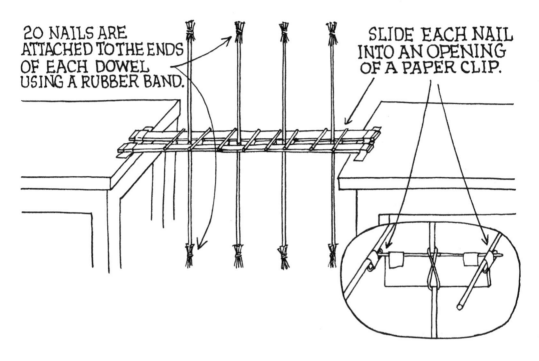

20 NAILS ARE ATTACHED TO THE ENDS OF EACH DOWEL USING A RUBBER BAND.

SLIDE EACH NAIL INTO AN OPENING OF A PAPER CLIP.

Step 9. Using the markings on the support structure yardsticks, move the 4 dowels to the 5-inch, 13-inch, 21-inch, and 29-inch marks. This will space the dowels 8 inches apart. (The other cross dowels will have to be repositioned to hold these long dowels at these points.)

Step 10. Cut 2 rubber bands and tie them together to form a single 10-inch piece. Make a total of 3 of these rubber-band connectors.

Step 11. Tie an end of the rubber-band connector to an end dowel about halfway down from the *pivot point* (the point from which the dowel swings). Tie the other end to the next dowel. Keep going until all the dowels are connected. When they are connected, the dowels should hang straight and there should be no slack in the rubber bands.

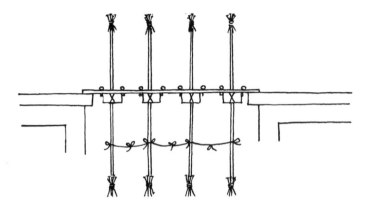

## Experiments to Try

The rubber-band connectors allow energy to pass through the dowels, so that moving a single dowel moves them all. In these experiments, you will move the rubber bands to different locations and change the weights on the dowels. After you have done a few experiments, see if you can predict the outcome of your next experiment.

Make sure the rubber-band connectors are in the right places throughout your experiments. The swinging of the dowels will cause them to move.

• Make sure the rubber-band connectors are in position A.

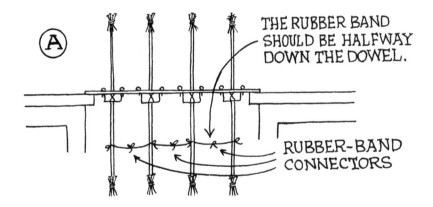

THE RUBBER BAND SHOULD BE HALFWAY DOWN THE DOWEL.

RUBBER-BAND CONNECTORS

Push a dowel. As it swings, watch how the others move. Do this several times to see if the same pattern occurs. One at a time, move the other dowels from the bottom and observe the movement.

• Make all the rubber-band connectors a little tighter. Move an end dowel and watch what happens.

• Make all the rubber-band connectors loose enough to hang slightly slack. Move an end dowel and watch what happens.

The 4 dowels can be connected to one another in a variety of ways. Here are some suggestions. Remember to use the same length rubber-band connector between the dowels.

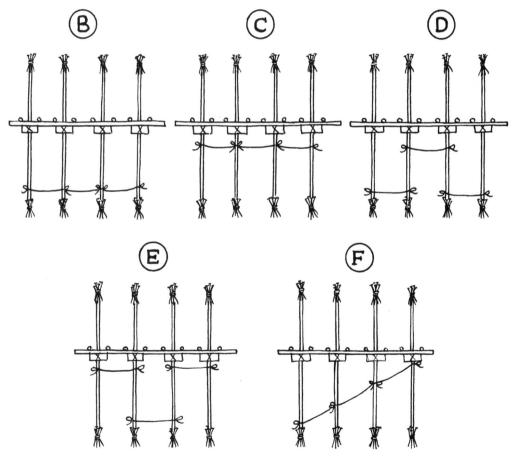

- Experiment with each position, moving a single dowel at a time. How does the placement of the rubber-band connectors affect the swinging of the dowels?
- With the rubber-band connectors in position A, make the weights at the bottom of the dowels unequal by using more or fewer nails. Swing each dowel individually. How does the unequal weight affect the movement of the dowels?

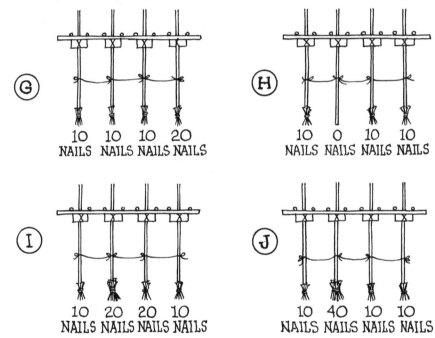

G
10 10 10 20
NAILS NAILS NAILS NAILS

H
10 0 10 10
NAILS NAILS NAILS NAILS

I
10 20 20 10
NAILS NAILS NAILS NAILS

J
10 40 10 10
NAILS NAILS NAILS NAILS

**What's Happening?**

When you change either the position of the rubber-band connectors or the amount of weight on the ends, the dowels move in a different pattern.

The farther away the rubber-band connectors are from the pivot point, as in position B, the more quickly the movement will be transferred from any dowel to another. The opposite happens when the rubber-band connectors are closer to the pivot, as in position C. It will take longer before the movement travels from the starting point to the other end. When the rubber-band connectors are lined up as in positions D or E, you get a type of dance. Moving the 2 left dowels first causes them to move together for a while before the 2 right dowels start to move. The movement goes back and forth between the 2 pairs. If you move the 2 right dowels, the energy is quickly transferred to the 2 left dowels and the exchange of energy between the sets of dowels occurs quickly. In position F, the dowel on the far right will move a number of times before the dowel on the far left moves. On the other hand, moving the dowel on the far left causes a quicker transfer of energy, so the other dowels move sooner.

When the number of nails at the bottom of the dowels is changed, the general rule is that the heavier dowel swings back and forth longer than the lighter ones. Swinging the dowel on the far right in position G will cause the one next to it to swing as high or even higher. This in turn passes the energy on to the others. However, it takes a longer time to transfer the energy back to the dowel with the 20-nail weight packet than for the 20-nail packet to transfer its energy to the 10-nail weight packet.

When a dowel is unweighted, as in position H, that dowel will swing wildly during the energy transfer—as much as the weighted dowels next to it. When more nails are added to the dowels, as in positions I and J, an unequal transfer happens. In position I, swinging an outer dowel results in a slower exchange of energy to the middle dowels. In position J, swinging either of the 2 dowels with 10-nail weight packets results in a similar action.

Changing the tension of the rubber-band connectors can also affect the rate at which energy is exchanged. The tighter the rubber-band connection, the more quickly the movement travels to the next dowel. The looser the connection, the slower the energy is exchanged.

You can now see how weight and flexibility affect the movement of energy across connected material. Making a stronger connection, whether by tightening the rubber bands or moving them closer to the ends of the dowels, allows a faster exchange of energy. Increasing the weight slows down the energy transfer.

# WAVE MACHINE #3: TWO CONNECTED DOWELS

In the last activity, 4 connected dowels produced many patterns of movement. Even after watching the swinging dowels for some time, it was probably hard for you to predict what would happen when you moved the rubber-band connectors or changed the weight on the dowels. In wave machine #2, there always seemed to be more than a single dowel moving, so it was not clear how much energy was being exchanged from one to another.

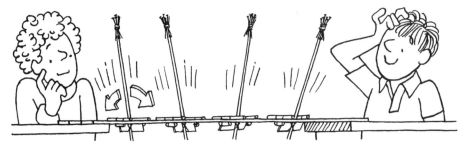

To better understand the energy exchange and predict what will happen when changes are made, you can use a wave machine that has only 2 connected dowels. If you are careful with your construction and your observations, you will begin to see clearer patterns of movement, and you will be able to count the swings more easily.

You will need:

        wave machine #2 (See pages 81–86 for assembly directions.)
        masking tape

Step 1.   Remove 2 rubber-band connectors from wave machine #2, so only 2 dowels are connected.

Step 2.   Put 20-nail weight packets securely on the top and bottom of each of the connected dowels.

Step 3. Put a small mark on the floor right underneath one of the connected dowels. Measure 10 inches from this point in front of the 2 dowels and put a small piece of masking tape on the floor to mark the spot.

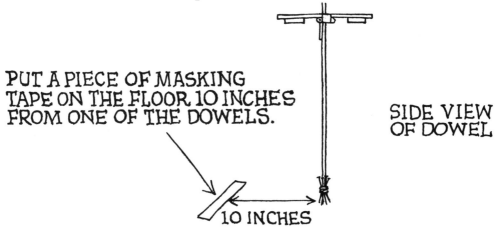

PUT A PIECE OF MASKING TAPE ON THE FLOOR 10 INCHES FROM ONE OF THE DOWELS.

SIDE VIEW OF DOWEL

10 INCHES

**Experiments to Try**

• Start with the rubber-band connector right above the weight packets. Pull a dowel out over the tape mark on the floor. Release the dowel and count the number of times it swings before it stops. Count the number of times the second dowel swings before it stops. Record your results.

• Move the rubber-band connector 1 inch higher on the dowels. Swing a dowel and count the number of times the second dowel swings before it stops.

• Keep moving the rubber-band connector 2 inches higher at a time and count the number of swings the second dowel makes before it stops. After a few times, try to guess how many times the second dowel will swing when the rubber band is 8 inches above the weight packets. Is there a point where the rubber band is so high that the dowel you pull does not transfer any energy to the second dowel?

• What happens when you add nails to a dowel and swing the other? How many times does the heavier dowel swing before it stops?

## What's Happening?

When 2 dowels of equal weight are connected, the movement of energy back and forth between them is usually regular. One swings a number of times and stops. The second swings about the same number of times, and then it stops. But the swinging of the second dowel sets the first moving again, and the movement becomes a series of cycles. In each cycle, the swings are lower, and there are fewer of them.

The lower the rubber-band connector is on the dowels, the more quickly the energy passes from dowel to dowel. As the rubber-band connector is moved up, there is a point where it is so high that no energy transfers. Pulling a dowel will move the other only a little, if at all. This is because the rubber-band connector is not stretched so far in the high position as in the low one.

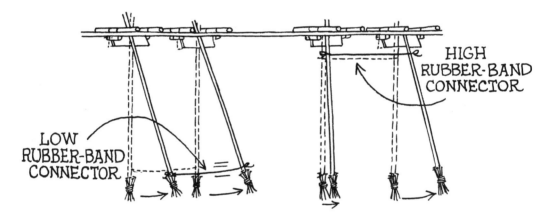

When you add extra weight to a dowel and start it swinging, it transfers its energy quickly to the lighter dowel. But when you swing the lighter dowel first, it will take longer for this dowel to transfer its energy to the heavier one.

By reducing the wave machine to 2 connected dowels, you are able to see much more consistent and predictable results. What you are seeing is energy transfer at its simplest.

# WAVE MACHINE #4: ONE DOWEL

In wave machine #1, many dowels were used. Changing some of the characteristics, such as the weight on the ends of the dowels, changed how energy was transferred from one dowel to another. With wave machines #2 and #3, it became easier to see patterns of movement and make fairly accurate predictions.

The next step is to examine how a single dowel moves back and forth and responds to changes. This device, wave machine #4, is called the *simple pendulum*. Its movement was first given special attention by one of the world's great scientists, Galileo Galilei (1564–1642). It is said that one day while attending church, he became interested in the candle fixtures that hung from long chains. Sometimes these fixtures were set slightly in motion by air currents. Galileo decided to time these swings with his own pulse, counting as he watched the moving fixtures.

Later he set up more careful experiments and eventually developed a precise mathematical formula that he could use to predict how changing one characteristic at a time, such as weight or length, would change the pattern of movement. You can carry out some of Galileo's experiments and see where his formulas came from.

You will need:

> wave machine #3, with all rubber-band connectors removed
> (See pages 90–91 for assembly directions.)
> a clock or wristwatch with a second hand

**Experiments to Try**

In the following experiments, make sure you change only a single
characteristic at a time. This is a good rule for experiments in
general, but it is especially important here. Remember to record
your results.

• Start with 10 nails attached to the bottom of the dowel. Pull the dowel
out to the mark on the floor and then let go. How long does it take to
make 15 swings?

• Add 5 more nails to the dowel. Pull it back to the mark and let go.
Now how long does it take for the dowel to swing 15 times?

• Continue to add 5 nails at a time to the bottom of the dowel and to
time 15 swings, until you have a total of 30 nails on the dowel. What
effect does adding weight have on the dowel?

• Remove 10 nails so there are now 20 on the dowel. Look at the notes
you made of your previous experiments and see how long it took for
a dowel with 20 nails on the bottom to swing 15 times. Move the 20
nails 5 inches higher on the dowel. Now how long do 15 swings take?
Keep moving up the nails, 5 inches at a time, and time 15 swings.
Continue until the nails are close to the pivot point.

**What's Happening?**

You may be surprised by your results as you add more and more nails
to the dowel. If you are careful in your experiments, you should have
discovered that the swing time doesn't change as you change the
weight. But moving the same weight closer and closer to the pivot
point makes the dowel swing faster and faster. If you started with a

94

much longer pendulum, moved the weights up the same distance each time, and then checked the different swing times, your results would still be regular and predictable.

This useful discovery led Galileo to the design of a new mechanical clock. At that time, clocks had falling weights that made the gears move. But it was hard to control the speed of the fall, so sometimes the hands moved too slowly, and sometimes too fast. Galileo proposed that a pendulum be used to regulate the clock's movements.

He wasn't able to make a practical working model from his design. However, some time later a Dutch scientist named Christian Huygens (1629–1695) did, and until recently some clocks still used this type of regulator.

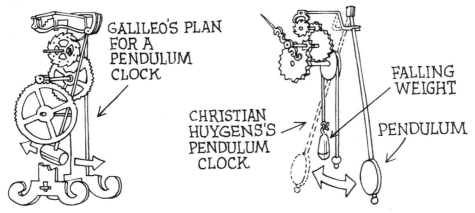

GALILEO'S PLAN FOR A PENDULUM CLOCK

CHRISTIAN HUYGENS'S PENDULUM CLOCK

FALLING WEIGHT

PENDULUM

As you saw, the model pendulum can move in a very predictable manner. In the previous investigation, you saw that 2 pendulums can act in a predictable manner. With 4 connected pendulums, you could predict their actions but the action was more complex.

Scientists attempt to analyze a complex phenomenon by starting with complicated systems and then trying to make them simpler. Calculations based on what is known about the simple pendulum and a few coupled pendulums help scientists understand and make predictions about such diverse phenomena as ocean waves, the transmission of sound, and the properties of light.

# THE SCIENCE OF WAVES

In the beginning of the book, you started out with a tank of water that modeled how waves might appear on the ocean or a lake. Then you changed the depth of the water to investigate how very thin materials might carry waves. This led to looking at waves in solid materials of different sizes, and you observed that they appear to behave in ways similar to waves in water. In the final sections, you saw how a collection of dowels could model wave motion and make it possible for scientists to control the variables and do systematic experiments.

As you progressed, your findings could be applied to more and more situations. This type of progression is what scientists are always striving for. They try to understand specific situations well and to see if they can be related in some way to other kinds of phenomena.

Sometimes a scientist's investigations produce interesting but isolated observations, like Galileo's idea for a more accurate clock. Then someone else, like Huygens, comes along and makes a connection. Eventually many observations are brought together under one system of explanation. This is what makes science fascinating and exciting. There are always new discoveries to be made, and new ways to think how these discoveries are related to ones in the past. Maybe you will come up with new discoveries that will add to the science of waves.